Mid-Life Directions

MID-LIFE DIRECTIONS

Praying and Playing
Sources of New Dynamism

Anne Brennan
Janice Brewi

PAULIST PRESS
New York/Mahwah

Library of Congress
Catalog Card Number: 84-62157

ISBN: 0-8091-2681-8

Published by Paulist Press
997 Macarthur Boulevard
Mahwah, N.J. 07430

Printed and bound in the United States of America

CONTENTS

INTRODUCTION

For eight years we have been giving Mid-Life Workshops, Seminars, Retreats. Together with more than 9,000 participants we've been encountering the dynamics of Mid-life crisis, the Mid-life transition and the lengthening period of Mid-life and the mature years. Each of these people has contributed to our knowledge and our growing awe of and fascination with the potentials of the Longevity Revolution for the flowering of each individual and humanity itself.

We believe that the "new frontier" is the development of personality in the Mid-life and Mature years. The growing life span and numbers of people in these stages after early adulthood and parenting years are a revelation pointing to the importance of the fullest development of each human spirit for the glory of God and the glory of the whole human project. A child born today must be able to look forward to life, liberty and the pursuit of happiness in the whole human journey he or she has embarked on, and this will only be true when that child can look forward to the aging process.

This book goes beyond our first book, *Mid Life Psychological and Spiritual Perspectives*, in focusing on the paradoxical wisdom of the Christian spiritual insight: "Unless you change and become like little children, you will not enter the Kingdom of God" (Mt 18:3) as a secret of new dynamism. The child prays and plays and so stoops to enter new life and unwitting, unimagined growth. Two thousand years ago, Jesus was in touch with a truth of human development that developmental psychologists and any of us touch today when we enter the deep down things of living.

In our reflections, the insights of Carl G. Jung have been a major influence. His empirical psychological perspective and the meaning perspective of Christian spiritual tradition have illumined one another to produce a further contribution to the development of a human and Christian spirituality for the second half of life. Inherent in and emerging from what in fact amounts to a second life span, a new gift of God to the human race in this perilous century is such a spirituality. It includes a call for a conversion of the use of human energy. As individuals and peoples our striving for ever more and more power, supremacy, control and wealth is a distortion of the striving for ego identity, will, roles and financial independence which were appropriate goals for the first half of life. We must be transformed into individuals and peoples who spend energy instead on the flowering of each unique human personality from the first moment of life and through all life stages to the last moment which promises a fulfillment and ratification beyond our wildest hopes.

CHAPTER 1

Individuation as a Life Goal

I. The Shadow—Gateway to Individuation

Individuation is the task of the second half of life. It refers to the process of adult growth as described by Carl G. Jung. The process of individuation is the process of self-knowledge, self-acceptance, ego-transcendence, interiorization and integration. The first half of life with its ego-building climate and activities is the necessary underpinning of the individuation movement that is the goal of the second half of life. It is a natural growth pattern within us but it can be stymied by our own culture and way of life. We need to cultivate our own growth. We need to understand the process of maturing within ourselves and others. We need to know what is involved in "coming to self-hood, self-realization, becoming an in-dividual."[1]

Scripture tells us that God made us in his own image and likeness.[2] To be made in the image and likeness of God means many things. It means that each of us has like God a uniqueness and individuality that is unparalleled. It means that like God we have a relationship with all of creation and all people. It means that like God goodness is the very core of our being. To be human is to be called to unfold the uniqueness of our own individuality. To be human is to be called to fully experience who we are and to creatively give that gift to the world. "The way of individuation is only the way when one finds it and follows it oneself."[3] The mid-life transition is an invitation to find and enter the way.

When does one cross the borderline between the first half of life and the second? Is there a clear demarcation for this second birth? It appears that in the first half of life each of us is named by the people, events, institutions that surround one. Imagine, each of us is called for a lifetime by the name given us at birth! We had no choice of parents, place or time, and no choice of name. Even more than the initial name, we were continually named thereafter by that environment. Our earliest self-concept stays with us as joy or pain throughout our life, no matter how modified or redeemed in later life. Perhaps one mark of the rebirth process is that miracle of moments when one freely chooses to live, to accept life, to be human, to accept the human situation. At this moment of acceptance I enter into the free and unconditional acceptance of my own life and becoming. I enter into bearing the tensions, the paradoxes of life. At this moment, each of us becomes equalized, for within each of us is the same polarity of good and evil.

James Carroll speaks of this human situation in his delightful story about a young princess who is going to take her life because she has discovered that she has a crack in her heart. At the same time a tumbler is leaving the kingdom. He too is afraid of pursuing his vocation because of a crack in his heart and the danger to his health that his vocation would cause. When he sees that the princess is about to end her life, he transcends his own fears and climbs up to save her. His courage allows him to see and he urges the princess to look down at the crowds of people. To her surprise each person has a crack in his heart.[4] The realization of our own weakness is not just arriving at our personal shadow but the shadow of the human race of which we are fully part. This is true solidarity and the realization of it is humbling and redeeming. No longer must we strive to be who we are not—perfect. Nor need we hide any aspect of ourself from Self. Eventually we come to say with Paul, "In my weakness is my strength." We no longer need to repress our shadow or project it upon others. We grow to understand the sinfulness of others because we have encountered and befriended it within ourselves.

Paul Tillich calls this essential self-affirmation of one's being "courage."[5] "Courage" fits this affirmation of Self because it is an act not done in blindness but in full realization of who it is I am affirming, of who it is I am saying yes to. In face "of those elements of his existence which conflict with his essential self-affirmation,"[6] that is knowing the truth about oneself, the good and the bad, I affirm myself. I say, "I do." This wedding with Self comes from deep within oneself. Now we are not being named by our outer environment, people, events, institutions. It is our inner environment—our own true Self—that graces us with full acceptance. When we take this step, when this miracle occurs, we have crossed the borderline. In every way it is a conversion, a new birth. It appears that we were born for this moment, and it initiates us into the process of the second half of life. That process is marked by a continual naming of ourselves by our inner environment. Not that we negate, castrate, the outer environment. Rather that our orientation is turned around. The "I" that one became in the first half of life is no longer in command. The Self that we were called to be, the unique individual that each of us is, slowly emerges and gradually takes over command. All the unconscious depths within us are to be discovered and to transform the naming of ourselves. We have wedded our Self for better or for worse, in good times and in bad. And this commitment is the threshold to the second half of life, to our second journey. This is why this transition is rightly called the "change of life." This is a genuine conversion, a movement of magnificient and earth shaking change. "The movement of conversion begins and ends in the acceptance of who we are."[7] This basic self affirmation that we are called to at the mid-point of our life is a call to conversion. It is an invitation to accept ourselves as we truly are, embracing our shadow and the dark side of ourselves, as well as embracing our good, all our possibilities and potentials and the mystery of our own being. In fact it is this genuine acceptance and love of Self that includes the good and the bad that is the key to genuine conversion because it is most God-like. This is how God loves us with full knowledge and acceptance, yet always calling us to go beyond who we are, our present image of ourself.

As a child, I always hated, felt uncomfortable with, angry about the "prodigal son" story. Secretly, I identified with the older son. I felt he had a right to be angry, jealous, put down. He had been good and faithful to the father. I too was angry that the father overlooked his goodness and was taken up with the younger son—gave him a party. I even thought a few times, "If that is how it is I may as well go out and do just as I damn please." It took me years to know that the younger son was lucky because he early encountered his own shadow. He early entered into true knowledge of self and the gateway to continual growth, individuation—that is, if he accepted and embraced that shadow. The older son identified himself with his ego strength striving for uprightness, fidelity to work and relationship. In this very striving he negated his opportunity for genuine relationship. His was the real selfishness. It prevented him from identifying with the Father's anguish and the Father's joy. It took many years of living as this "older son" before my eyes were opened to the truth. I was the prodigal. The younger son and older son were both prodigal in their own way. In my identification with my ego, my being good, honest, upright, selfless, I truly wasted all with egocentric living in disguise. I truly deserted the Father by not taking on who I really was and giving him all that. It was like a baptism, this awakening. It was a coming home to whole parts of me—long rejected. It was as though now the Father was throwing me a party because I had come home. I truly laughed to think that the younger son who so angered me was me in truth. Whether it is the early conflict of the younger son or the later conflict of the older son, in some way, and only in real life, do we each come to know our shadow and our true self.

Coming to accept the personal and non-personal shadow within ourselves is the gateway to continual growth. When we are young and trying to be good—good children, good parents, good friends, good wives and husbands, good professionals, good ministers—we cannot see the power for evil within ourselves as it would overcome us. We are not conscious of our impure motives, our selfishness, our ego-centeredness. How often have we done something for someone else and been unaware of the fact that it was for ourselves? Often what we did for someone's good was totally unconscious of the genuine needs of the other. We believe that we are good and are unconscious of our own motivations. Many of us live with our head in the sky and are unaware that our feet are in the clay. Jung tells us that this confrontation with the true self is the "first test of courage on the inner way."[8] Speaking of a woman he helped in dealing with this initial confrontation he says,

> She had, in her earlier development, lifted herself above the earth and was growing into the sky. But when such is the case the roots grow down into hell.[9]

The full acceptance of our humanity is the full acceptance of the power for good and evil that lies within us. If we are to be truly human we need to come to the point that when we look out from our prison bars we see the mud *as well as* the stars.

This initial confrontation humbles us and graces us with the gifts of mercy and forgiveness. We find mercy and forgiveness pouring out from our inner core toward others. Isn't that what happened to old Scrooge in *A Christmas Carol?* He saw himself with all his evil, as he really was. This knowledge moved him to be born again and he began to experience goodness from within and mercy, forgiveness and love to others. Transcending the darkness within ourself allows us to deal with our present culture and its institutions and the darkness within them. Like the psalmist we have the courage to say: "Even though I would walk in the dark valley I fear no evil; for you are at my side."[10]

Roger Gould, speaking of the mid-life crisis decade as the collapse of the final major false assumption of our life—"There is no evil or death in the world. The sinister has been destroyed"—comments on the process of our encounter with the evil within.

> To achieve an adult sense of freedom, we must pass through periods of passivity, rage, depression and despair as we experience the repugnance of death, the hoax of life and the evil within and around us. To enjoy full access to our innermost self, we can no longer deny the ugly, demonic side of life, which our immature mind tried to protect against by enslaving itself to false illusions.[11]

We have all heard that the ability to sleep is a sign of faith and trust in God. One woman who came to our mid-life workshop had not had a good night's sleep in months. She listened and participated in the first day's activity. We considered the phenomenon of mid-life itself. We explored what happened to us in the first half of life. We looked at our changing values and moved toward the movement of the next day: What do we want to do with tomorrow? When our friend returned the second day she esctactically exclaimed that she had had a good night's sleep! Yes, she perhaps had been moved to trust in God. We had prayed together and sung "Be Not Afraid." But she had been moved to trust also in the process of mid-life change and transition that she and her recently retired husband were going through. Of course trusting in God and trusting in life stages and change, the fruit of God's creative plan, are the same thing! In the second half of life, let us relax and sleep and above all let us learn again to play and pray. We are where we are, and realization and acceptance and faith in that will cultivate the unfolding of this moment. We can have no greater faith both in God and in the process of life we are in than the faith that is called forth in praying and playing. In both we let go of the determinations of the ego, we suspend this terrible seriousness of ours and we allow our Self to be for a time without a cause, without a goal. We are before the Lord, accepting where things are with ourselves, with the world, with the ones we love—letting it be; we pray and play. We have become like little children—ready to enter the Kingdom of heaven where the lion and lamb lay down together.[12] The way of individuation is the way of our ancestors. Hebrews tells us that we are pilgrims and sojourners as all our fathers were.[13] We come to realize in this confrontation with our shadow that we are only on the way. This gateway to the second half of life fills us with questions whereas before we had so many answers. We are filled with mystery whereas before we saw and knew all. We are searching, content not to have the prize.[14] In a sense we have become like little children. Once we have crossed the threshold on our way of individuation, once we have encountered our shadow, transcended and transformed our ego by activating the relationship of our conscious and unconscious we begin to ask again: Who am I really? What else is there about me that I am unaware of at this moment? What surprises await me? The archetypal Self appears as a friend demanding our time and emotional commitment. Speaking of the mid-life transition Daniel Levinson says

> In this period the archetypal Self takes on a greater definition and vitality. It becomes a more active internal figure, someone that the conscious ego must learn to talk with and listen to. . . . He must separate himself from the striving ego and the external pressures, so that he can better hear the voice from within.[15]

II. Heterosexual Consciousness

We each have within us so many potentials, untapped resources, sources of creativity seeking emergence at this time of our life. We come to realize that the "I" we thought we were is only part of who we really are. I myself can remember the intensity of the first six years of my religious life. I wanted so much to be all "I should be," to give all to God, to be a perfect nun. When at the close of those six years I made my final profession I had the thought, "Well, now I have nothing to do until I die. I've done it all. I've given all to God. I just have to wait until the end." How little I knew myself. Today, more than twenty years later, I am amazed at all that has awakened, and I know that there is so much within me not yet tapped. I have so many determinisms that I have not yet moved through and beyond. Individuation is the invitation to see more than the ego, the I that I am conscious of. It "is the process of the ego discovering, conversing with, and relating to the objective psyche, and realizing that it is subject to this more comprehensive psychic entity."[16] Each of us is more than the I.

Here are a few descriptions of the sense of "more than the ego" that participants of the mid-life workshop described.

> I've touched the surface of who I am. A whole new experience for me. I'm no longer only so and so's wife or so and so's Mom. I'm me.

> I don't know what went wrong. I worked hard—made more than a good living. Now the children are gone and we feel alone. They seem to resent us. There is no real warmth of relationship. We have gone for counseling. It has helped. I feel I've wasted the first half of my life and that I'm just beginning to awaken to the things that matter.

> My husband began his crisis about five years ago and the turmoil that this brought to our home was very great . . . . Now we are partners and friends, not just husband and wife and mother and father. I have begun my journey, and although the feelings and emotions are very frightening to me I now have someone to share them with. Just recently I told him that although it sounds very selfish—for the first time since I had been a teenager I felt a need to come first—to come before him or our daughter. To allow my needs to surface instead of always being suppressed or overshadowed by theirs.

> I have become aware of an evolution in my life. Until now I've been busy doing for youngsters and an ambitious husband. They're almost launched now and I feel like I'm standing on the dock watching them sail away. I'm looking for some direction to take myself when I step from the dock back to land.

> I came to realize I must have more of a balance in my daily life—no more work, work, work which pattern I was forced into by circumstances I couldn't change. Now I have to have more time doing whatever I choose.

The dissatisfaction, dis-ease, dis-contentment expressed by all these people is a sign of a call. It is a call to individuation, a call to explore the terrain of one's soul, and in that process the Self, so much more than the I (ego) emerges. It must be an exploration that leads to encounters. It is not enough to see the landscape of our hearts; we must experience it—be transformed by it—for the Self to emerge. The first encounter with our personal and non-personal shadow paves the way—even as the glaciers cut into the mountains a smooth path, a fertile valley. As we experience ourselves in this comprehensive way and a transformation of personality takes place, a new image emerges, naming ourself and our life experience as a totality. Reaching out beyond ourselves this new image allows us to see ourselves connected to God and to all creation. The emergence of a unifying symbol signifies the birth of a new attitude on our part: toward ourself and the world. Individuation is a call to become our own unique Self so that we have a Self to enter into relationship. "Individuation does not shut us out from the world, but gathers the world to oneself."[17]

Another way of seeing the task of mid-life individuation is simply as the task of resolving the conflicts of the polarities of life. Coming to our own shadow and even discovering within it a source of creativity and new life is part of the destruction/creation polarity that Daniel Levinson speaks about. The masculine/feminine polarity is another. ". . . every man at mid-life must come more fully to terms with the coexistence of masculine and feminine parts of the Self."[18] The polarities exist during the entire life cycle and are never fully resolved or transcended.[19] At mid-life they operate with a specific force and demand greater attention and integration. Ann Ulanov reminds us that as we mature "integration increasingly has more to do with recovering an inner value than with establishing outer order."[20]

Most of us have developed a strong masculinity or femininity during the first half of life. Yet within the breadth of the human experience each person is called to both masculine and feminine experiences. The mid-life transition calls for an acceptance of the contra-sexual within ourselves. Jung calls it the "anima" within the man and the "animus" within the woman. Despite the fact that we are at ease with our masculine or feminine way of adapting, we experience inner eruptions of the opposite within us. The man longs for close relationships. He questions for the first time in his life—hours of drinking with the boys, emotional energy given to a company or industry that may soon eject him, a wife he feels he can neither leave nor love. He is being called to look within and discover his own feminine counterpart. In fear he may project upon another woman, a sweet young thing, or an intelligent, energetic, sexy, exciting woman the feminine self, he runs away from. Unaware of all of this he may grow moody, despondent, depressed. He is being called to activate whole other areas of his personality, and the refusal to enter into this confrontation causes havoc. Both projection and repression of the feminine will cause an unhealthy and unbecoming entrance of the anima whether he likes it or not. What can be done? Whatever the eruptions are that he is experiencing, the question must be asked: What is this telling me?

Perhaps he could begin by starting a correspondence with the neglected feminine aspect of himself. Such a correspondence could strengthen the heterosexual reality of his own psyche. He should correspond with his anima as he would with any woman. Perhaps he has never corresponded with a woman. Perhaps he has never felt free or comfortable with a woman. He may have been overpowered by women in his life. It could be that deep down he does not feel truly masculine. He may feel he is being called to befriend his feminine and he has never truly befriended his masculine. Still he may have an abhorrence for the feminine and see it as weak, immature, unpredictable and sentimental. With the whole culture he may have fallen prey to "the denigration of qualities and attitude thought to be feminine."[21] He may have taken on the sexism of our culture and its corresponding "complex of myths and concepts rationalizing male dominance."[22] The turmoil he feels is a command to enter into an appreciation of the feminine, to enjoy the complementarity of male and female within himself. He must enter into serious dialogue with his feminine about all of this. But can he enter into serious dialogue with someone who is a non-entity or whom he despises? If not, he will never discover the importance of the inner subjective world. The feminine aspect of himself will not shipwreck his masculinity but wants to be integrated into that conscious masculine attitude, thus transforming it and making it even more masculine with the beauty of the feminine. He may encounter his anima in dreams, and sexual dreams at this time of life may have more to do with his anima than with eroticism.

Women at this time also have a need to discover and befriend their masculine side. Deep within each of us are the archetypal images of masculine and feminine. These images or patterns of being and relating may be encrusted in our personal experience of men and women who played a part in our early life, but underneath this shell are the archetypal patterns that are the inheritance of humanity. The images, more than personal, when released can counteract a poor, deficient, or warped masculine or feminine model that we experienced in childhood. When the masculine image is awakened in a woman, her old way of adapting is challenged. If she allows the masculine to surface and to be integrated into her conscious personality, a transformation takes place. Earlier the masculine qualities appeared to be in contradiction and opposition to the feminine adaptive attitude that had been here—now they give witness to being complementary. It is usually not a smooth transition. Sometimes a woman's femininity is shipwrecked as she struggles to open herself to this new dimension. But this pain and conflict can foster a mediation between the ego and the unconscious masculine self looking for an outlet. This mediation is pure gold. She too can awake and confirm this mediation by carrying on a dialogue with her animus, or masculine self. It will bless her with a renewed, awakened and more creative personality. Such a woman in the second half of life is seen growing even more feminine and womanly in her new-found objectivity, emotional confidence and ability to resonate a strength and vigor that comes from within.

The anima or animus within us is as much a part of our objective psyche as our legs and heart are a part of our physical being. Both the masculine and feminine within us have key contributions to make in our personality development. We should at this time in our life (mid-life) feel comfortable enough with our masculinity or femininity to allow the opposite to begin to take an active part in who we are becoming. Earlier in life these polarities would have been in such contradiction to each other that it would have been impossible to imagine their integration. As a man integrates his feminine into his personality there is no longer any need to project upon others this aspect of himself. We need no longer make idols of each other or devils or witches. Our society, having rejected the feminine qualities, is also in pain because of this dormant, neglected, despised self. The renewal of society in our day calls for a confrontation and integration of the anima. Men and women who have embraced both sides themselves will be the ones to bring about this renewal.

> The man who thinks you can be either a man, all man, or a woman, and nothing but a woman, is doomed to struggle with himself, and to external estrangement from women. To the extent that he learns the facts of psychological "bisexuality" and becomes aware of the arbitrariness of either/or definitions and the pathogenic nature of the process of dichotomizing, to the degree that he discovers that differences fuse and are structured with each other, and need not be exclusive and mutually antagonistic, to that extent will he be a more integrated person, able to accept and enjoy the "feminine" within himself. . . . If he can make peace with the female inside, he can make peace with the female outside, understand them better, be less ambivalent about them, and even admire them more as he realizes how superior their femaleness is to his own weaker version. You can certainly communicate better with a friend who is appreciated and understood than you can with a feared, resented, and mysterious enemy. To make friends with some portion of the outside world, it is well to make friends with that part of it which is within yourself.[23]

III. Owning and Transcending Our Typology

For all of us it appears that some external event thrust us into the mid-life crisis/transition.[24] Carl G. Jung's break with his colleague and mentor Sigmund Freud was the external event that precipitated his own mid-life crisis/transition.

> After the parting of the ways with Freud, a period of inner uncertainty began for me. It would be no exaggeration to call it a state of disorientation. I felt totally suspended in mid-air, for I had not yet found my footing.[25]

This disorientation was for Jung, as it is for all of us an invitation to pursue the discovery of his own true Self. He too had spent the first half of his life "primarily" adapting to the outer world. Now his strong disagreements with Freud were a healthy encounter with himself and a call to become the unique Self that he was. The pain of the disagreement and the isolation it caused him threw him into a search for understanding what had happened. He found it "necessary to study the polarity and dynamics of the psyche."[26] In 1921 he published *Psychological Types*, the fruit of his long study and investigation of the root causes for that most painful yet blessed separation. Here he discusses the four aspects or functions of consciousness: thinking/feeling, intuiting/sensing by which a person relates to the world, self, persons and things, and the two attitudes of consciousness: introversion/extroversion. Here he portrays for us the conclusion or insight that he came to "that every judgment made by an individual is conditioned by his personality type and that every point of view is necessarily relative."[27] This awakening for Jung brought to a close the personal healing of his alienation with Freud. Once he was able to see that the root cause was a universal problem of type he was freed from the disruptive effects of that alienation and it became a creative source of his own personal growth and of his psychology of types for all of us.

Just as the first half of life is for the development of our ego or conscious self, the first half of life is also for the development of our own unique typology. We may share that typology with billions of others but it will be uniquely our own and expressed in the first and second half of life in our own most original way. Our typology flows from a cluster of opposites: introversion/extroversion, thinking/feeling, intuiting/sensing. It appears that we all have a natural inborn tendency toward executing one of each of these pairs.[28] Nevertheless we each have a capacity to operate with each of the six. A healthy personality in the first half of life tends toward an unconscious selection or natural aptitude in one of each pair. Just as a natural selection or preference is important for ego development in the first half of life, a realization of the fact that the opposites of our natural selections are also part of our unconscious personality and therefore our undeveloped Self is a key to growth and flowering in the second half of life.

The individuation process which calls for an integration of the unconscious with the conscious demands a surfacing of the opposite pole of our natural selection and a rapprochement of the two. Once again it is not a case of one usurping or replacing the other but of the ego typology being transformed by the Self which demands that respect be given to the unconscious functions and attitudes. Jung's typology in a sense is a road map to understand where we traveled in the first half of life—the road of extroversion or introversion, the path of thinking or feeling, sensing or intuiting. It is a road map for the second half of life as it suggests that for our full development we need appreciation not only for our first and natural selection but for the shadow side that has been neglected and now wants to make some real contribution to our knowledge and enjoyment of the outer and inner world.

An image of introversion and extroversion is found in the two different kinds of responses of new-born babies. Whether or not it actually reflects their attitude toward consciousness or not, it does give us an image of the introverted and extroverted attitude. Some infants when placed upon their mother's stomachs immediately following birth, before the umbilical cord is cut, cuddle up in a fetal position and lie quiet and content, while other infants immediately reach out with hands and feet both squealing and squirming. We each have to deal with our inner world and our outer world if we are to survive in our human journey, but all of us tend to have a natural aptitude for dealing with one over the other; one of those two worlds seems to draw our psychic energy. There is an unconscious attraction and aversion for one or the other. They are both like an inner and outer climate and both are seducing us, one poorly and one expertly. So true is this that it takes half of our life to realize how and by whom we have been seduced. Now at the mid-life transition time the charms of the other seducer begin to surface. We have the dual task of consciously accepting our primary seducers and appreciating how they helped us to develop and relate and the unique contribution they made to the original person we have become and at the same time paying attention to the losers and letting them, to a degree, become successful enchantresses.

> When psychopathology develops in the first half of life it usually expresses the failure to establish a firm hold on external adaptation and to achieve a realistic ego development through making the most of one's superior functions. In the second half of life, from the forties on, danger arises

> when not enough attention is paid to the inadequate functions which now press for admittance, even though our lives may be satisfactorily adapted in terms of external reality.[29]

Many an introvert longs for the balancing of extroversion and vice versa. Here it is important for caution, and we would do well to remember this wise saying, "Make new friends but keep the old; one is silver and the other gold." Thinking and feeling, sensing and intuiting, once in opposition, now long for one to balance the other. We discover that our greatest gifts, virtues, talents and charisms flow from our natural selection or typology as well as our greatest conflicts, pains, struggles, and disorientations. We begin to see how relative our way of perceiving and judging is and open ourself to people with the opposite and the dormant capacity for the same within us. We begin to appreciate the unique contribution we can make with our perceptive and judgment functions to situations and to people who have buried within themselves what has become our mode of being. We are humbled, knowing that our inferior function—the opposite of our primary function—has been the cause of so much personal and communal conflict in our daily life. We can befriend our inferior function as children befriend each other in play. Sometimes in play our inferior function becomes a most seductive influence almost overwhelming our ego. Just as this neglected aspect of ourself was the source of so many curses, she can now become the source of genuine ecstasy. The thinker whose primitive feeling is aroused is overcome just as the feeler who for the first time has logic, objective, analytical thought erupt in the midst of a judgment taking on the impact of striking oil. The intuitive, continually inundated with ideas, feeding on them, ecstatically moving from one to the other, is overwhelmed by the bodily senses when they occasionally erupt and subdue and replace for a time the usual intuitive bombardment. The sensing function so demanding for the factual climax of all five ways of dealing with and perceiving things (the senses) is likewise drowned out by the occasional intuition or hunch that overpowers the natural exercise of demand for sensing. In all these cases, the unknown, and seldom if ever experienced, takes on a numinous quality, a once in a lifetime effect that can intoxicate us but also give us a taste of the other side of the mountain. We are transformed in their experience if we accept them as a challenge to open us to the genuine values of our inferior parts and invite them to surface and then begin to integrate them into our conscious typology.

The process of coming to terms with our inferior function is paramount to our growth in wholeness, and Jung called it the "transcendent function."[30] The transcendent function unites the pairs of opposites within us. It transcends their in-built opposition and rejection of each other. This is the goal of individuation the integration of all our diverse parts into the unique Self, the whole Self we were meant to be from the start. The person in the process of individuation can foster the individuation of society. Respect among religions, Christians, nations, and people of all kinds and true human community can only come about when we have each learned to respect our own divergent parts and appreciate their contribution to our own wholeness.

IV. Individuation—Conversion Frontier

Individuation is a natural process, the goal of a lifetime. It is an invitation to the journey toward maturity, wholeness, differentiation and integration. Refusal to change to confront the unknown, to bear the tension of opposites, to allow new experiences to come to consciousness, to see ourselves as more than we are can and will hinder the growth process. Because individuation is a process it is never a finished product but always "a movement toward." "Individuation like conversion—is to be seen as a direction of movement rather than as a once-for-all completed fact."[31]

Individuation is a conversion because it demands a complete turnabout. Whereas in the first half of life we struggled to build a strong identity and ego in order to deal with, live in, and adapt to the outer world, we are now called to relativize that ego. We are asked to admit into our consciousness whole other areas of our unconscious personality that are in opposition to our ego and to allow that confrontation to give birth to the Self. The Self becomes the central force of our lives. Speaking of such a conversion in the real lives of individuals, Bernard Lonergan says:

> It is not merely a change or even a development; rather, it is a radical transformation on which follows, on all levels of living, an interlocked series of changes and developments.

> What hitherto was unnoticed becomes vivid and present. What had been of no concern becomes a matter of high import. So great a change in one's apprehensions and one's values accompanies no less a change in oneself, in one's relation to other persons, and in one's relation to God.[32]

Individuation is a spiritual or religious response or engagement with life itself. Jung realized that just as personal problems in the first half of life were related to our adaptation to the outer life, personal problems in the second half of life were always related to adaptation to our inner life, our own depths.

> Among all my patients in the second half of life—that is to say, over thirty five—there has not been one whose problem in the last resort was not that of finding a religious outlook on life.[33]

To leave behind the ego-centered familiar worldly empire of our long fought for and hard struggled youthful energies and to go beyond all that to the unknown inner depths of Self is to go upon a religious quest. It is to be like Abraham and to go in search of a new horizon at the command of the Lord. Like Abraham we are asked to sacrifice our only son, our prized and cherished ego. Paradoxically our very willingness to do so accomplishes the task without the death of the ego. The ego lives as Isaac lived and enters into the process of giving birth to the Self as it throws itself into the contractions of confrontation not annihilation.

Individuation is precipitated by an inner or outer turmoil from which we have no recourse or alleviation. With our first birth there were natural signs. Every mother knows what to look for: the timing of contractions, the breaking of the water. Puberty brings with it an amazing number of sacramental signs of a coming psychic birth or change. Adolescent turmoil creates a vivid portrayal of the breaking away that is necessary before you can come into your own. In the same way, one finds oneself thrown into the turmoil that in a sense is the breaking up of the ground for the planting of the seed and the "third birth" into mid-life.

> One thing is sure, no one will ever begin the journey by free choice, without some inner pressure. Some dynamics

> have to be at work. Anything can be instrumental. Something disturbing happens to upset the balance in one's life, so that one feels exposed to chaotic forces one cannot master. In answer, in compensation to these, the urge for self-determination stirs.[34]

This is the mid-life crisis, an invitation to become more than we are. It is an invitation to become the unique Self we were born to become. There never was a birth without pain. But there are ways of birthing that can transcend the pain of the birthing process and double the joy at the end.

Individuation is a call to relativity.

> Just as before, perhaps, neurotic disorders arose because the opposing fantasies were unconscious, so now other disorders arise through the repression of former idols. It is of course a fundamental mistake to imagine that when we see the non-value in a value or the untruth in a truth, the value or the truth ceases to exist. It has only become relative. Everything human is relative, because everything rests on an inner polarity, for everything is a phenomenon of energy.[35]

There is great danger at this time in our life when we are becoming dissatisfied with, alientated from our "I" that we change our "angels" into "devils" and our "devils" into "angels." Values that are no longer satisfying and appear now to be deceptive become despised and rejected. What formerly was despised and rejected appears to be desirable, valuable, angelic. Instead of enduring the conflict of opposites, instead of bearing the tensions allowing the opposing values to confront each other, we collapse one side of the polarity. This can result in living in complete opposition to our former ego—not in uniting the ego (conscious) and unconscious. "Changes of profession, divorces, religious convulsions, apostasies of every description, are the symptoms of this swing to the opposites."[36]

Individuation is a prerequisite for genuine true community. Only individuals can enter into community. Individuation is the process of becoming the unique individual we were meant to be. When I can bring my individuality, uniqueness and potential wholeness to a group or another person, I can hope for unity with differentiation—that is, community. This is the only kind of unity possible in the second half of life. Marital problems, relationship problems with individuals, churches, organizations, groups, institutions at this time in our life may be a struggle for life itself. We need to grow, to differentiate ourself from others. We need to become an individual in order to be able to be a communion. To give an example, Max Zeller tells us:

> Behind a couple's constant fighting may be hidden a tendency towards separation, not in the sense of splitting up the relationship, but a psychological separation for the sake of a creative more individual development in both of them, which in turn would lead to a true relationship.[37]

It appears that individuation is the call to a potential unity of Self and is the first step toward unity with those we love, unity with all of creation and unity with God.

Individuation is the call of Christ: "Come, follow me." Come and respond to the Spirit within and without yourself. Come and respond to the consciousness and growth in awareness. Come and respond to the revelation of the first half of life as I did. Come and be true to your own insights, your inner depths as I was. This invitation of Christ to each of us is an invitation to life itself. Come to trust and love your Self and all its parts, conscious and unconscious, known and unknown. When you respond to this invitation you enter into the process of conversion, the process of individuation. The heavens are opened and you hear within your inner depths: "This is my beloved in whom I am well pleased." You have been born again by the power of the Spirit. Difficult times lie ahead of you—but you have put your hand to the plow and cannot turn back. Like Jesus, you will be led into the desert and you too will have to face up to the most terrifying temptations. Just as this time marked the transition between the life of Jesus of Nazareth and Jesus the Son of Man, reality of the Kingdom, which he was born to be, so too we will find that as our Self emerges we too are becoming the one we were born to be. To be that self even though it brings rejection, death on a cross is the goal of our life and anticipates our coming glory. For all of us the mid-life transition is a call to respond to the Spirit as Jesus did. It is a religious way of life. It becomes for all of us the turning point of our lives. "Some kind of conversion, while desirable at any age, is a must upon entrance to the middle years . . . that this is the great "conversion" frontier and that much of our previous thinking about conversion must be altered to heed the work of the Spirit in the thirties and forties."[38]

Notes

1. C.G. Jung, *Two Essays on Analytical Psychology*, trans. R.F.C. Hull, 2nd edition, Bollingen Series XX, The Collected Works of C.G. Jung, Vol. 7 (Princeton, New Jersey: Princeton University Press, 1966), p. 173.
2. Gen 1:26a.
3. C.G. Jung, *The Integration of the Personality*, trans. Stanley Dell (New York: Farrar and Rinehart, Inc., 1939), p. 32.
4. James Carroll, "The Tumbler and the Princess," *Wonder and Worship* (New York: Paulist Press, 1970), pp. 133–138.
5. Paul Tillich, *The Courage To Be* (New Haven: Yale University Press, 1952), p. 3.
6. *Ibid.*
7. Jacques Pasquier, "Experience & Conversion," *Conversion*, ed. Walter E. Conn, Ph.D. (New York: Alba House 1978), pp. 191–200.
8. C.G. Jung, "The Integration of the Personality," p. 69.
9. *Ibid.*, p. 39.
10. Ps 23:4.
11. Roger L. Gould, *Transformations* (New York: Simon and Schuster, 1978), p. 218.
12. Is 11:6.
13. Heb 11:3.
14. Heb 12:1.
15. Daniel J. Levinson, *The Seasons of a Man's Life* (New York: Knopf, 1978), p. 241.
16. Ann Belford Ulanov, *The Feminine In Jungian Psychology and in Christian Theology* (Evanston: Northwestern University Press, 1971), p. 71.
17. C.G. Jung, *On the Nature of the Psyche*, trans. R.F.C. Hull, Bollingen Series, third printing (Princeton: Princeton University Press, 1973), p. 136.

18. Daniel Levinson, *The Seasons of a Man's Life*, p. 197.

19. *Ibid.*, p. 198.

20. Ann Belford Ulanov, *The Feminine in Jungian Psychology and in Christian Theology*, p. 71.

21. Edmund J. Egan, "The Transformation of Ethics and Heterosexual Consciousness," *Cross Currents*, Summer 1973, p. 170.

22. *Ibid.*, p. 177.

23. Abraham Maslow, *The Farther Reaches of Human Nature* (New York: The Viking Press, 1972), p. 162.

24. Gerald O'Collins, *The Second Journey* (New York: Paulist Press, 1978).

25. Carl G. Jung, *Memories, Dreams and Reflections*, trans. Richard and Clara Winston, recorded and ed. by Aniella Jaffe (New York: Random House, 1961; Vintage Books Paperback, 1965).

26. *Ibid.*, p. 155.

27. *Ibid.*, p. 207.

28. C.G. Jung, *Modern Man in Search of a Soul*, trans. W.S. Dell and Cary F. Baynes (New York: Harvest Book, Harcourt, Brace and World Inc., 1933), p. 80.

29. Edward C. Whitmont, *The Symbolic Quest* (Princeton: Princeton University Press, 1969), p. 147.

30. C.G. Jung, *Mysterium Coniunctionis*, trans. R.F.C. Hull (New Jersey: First Princeton/Bollingen Paperback, 1977), p. 200.

31. Seward Hiltner, "Toward a Theology of Conversion in the Light of Psychology," *Conversion*, ed. Walter E. Conn, Ph.D. (New York: Alba House, 1978), p. 179.

32. Bernard Lonergan, "Theology in Its New Context," *Conversion*, ed. Walter E. Conn, Ph.D. (New York: Alba House, 1978), p. 13.

33. C.G. Jung, *Modern Man in Search of a Soul*, p. 264.

34. Max Zeller, "Some Aspects of the Individuation Process," Paper No. 10 (Los Angeles: The Analytical Psychology Club of Los Angeles Inc., May 1960), p. 3.

35. C.G. Jung, "Two Essays on Analytical Psychology," p. 75.

36. *Ibid.*

37. Max Zeller, "Some Aspects of the Individuation Process," p. 5.

38. Seward Hiltner, "Toward a Theology of Conversion in the Light of Psychology," p. 190.

CHAPTER 2

The Unconscious in the Personality Theory of Carl Jung

I. Toward the Unconscious

In his eighty-third year, a short time before his death, Carl Jung wrote his autobiography. That testament, entitled *Memories, Dreams, Reflections*, begins with a statement about the supreme importance of the unconscious, not only in his psychological theory but in his life. The Prologue begins:

> My life is a story of the self-realization of the unconscious. Everything in the unconscious seeks outward manifestation and the personality too desires to evolve out of its unconscious conditions and to experience itself as a whole.[1]

A page later he expands on the same thought:

> Recollection of the outward events of my life has largely faded or disappeared. But my encounters with the "other" reality, my bouts with the unconscious, are indelibly ingrained upon my memory. In that realm there has always been wealth in abundance, and everything else has lost importance by comparison. . . . I early arrived at the insight that when no answer comes from within to the problems and complexities of life, they ultimately mean very little. Outward circumstances are no substitute for inner experience.[2]

These words from a creative genius, one of the fathers of modern psychology, healer of thousands, friend and acquaintance of most of the famous and influential figures of the early twentieth century, author of hundreds of works, artist, scientist, scholar, seems to turn some significant Western values inside out. How impossible it seems that all these accomplishments are pale. How could his life be only a "wrestling with the unconscious"? How could his life be but "inner experience"? As one studies the life and work of Carl Jung however, the seeming contradiction in his perception disappears. It becomes immensely clear that his greatest contribution to the modern world is his returning to it its soul precisely in his vision and explorations of the unconscious. How true that all his healing, his influence, his scholarship, all his writings and art and most of all his own vibrant personality were all expressions of his perception of and relationship with the unconscious.

> His overwhelming contribution to psychological understanding is his concept of the unconscious—not like the unconscious of Freud, merely a gory hole of repressed desires, but a world that is just as much vital and real a part of the life of the individual as the conscious "cogitating" world of the ego, and infinitely wider and richer. The language and "people" of the unconscious are symbols and the means of communication, dreams.[3]

Jung had several experiences in his childhood which he was much later to name experiences of the unconscious. In his autobiography the eighty-three year old Jung recalls the three or four year old little boy that he once was dreaming of a phallic deity underground, and he recalls himself as a twelve year old drifting off into the unconscious in a neurotic way. The grandeur, the vastness and the power and danger of the unconscious to which such experiences introduced him became two of the great pillars of his approach to the unconscious. The reality of the unconscious for him, even in his boyhood, is further emphasized in his sense of himself as being two different personalities: a number one personality, the schoolboy, and a number two personality, someone old and venerable who knew some of God's great secrets.

The earliest dream that Jung could recall was one which preoccupied him all his life, though he never spoke of it until he was sixty-five years old. In the dream, he found a dark, rectangular, stone-lined hole in the ground. He descended and found a golden throne. On it was a large phallic symbol with an eye in it. The dream terrified him and became the psychic backdrop to his later experiences of religion. Whenever after he heard about the mild Christ from his mother or his minister father or in religious instruction, there was always this counterpoint image of the awesome underground god. He asks in his autobiography:

> Who spoke to me then: Who talked of problems far beyond my knowledge? Who brought the Above and Below to-

> gether and laid the foundation for everything that was to fill the second half of my life with stormiest passion? Who but that alien guest who came both from above and from below? Through this childhood dream I was initiated into the secrets of the earth. . . . My intellectual life had its unconscious beginning at that time.[4]

At twelve, shoved and knocked down by another boy Jung's head was struck. Half-conscious, he remembered thinking, "Now you won't have to go to school anymore."[5] For more than six months he did stay away from school—free, dreaming, drawing, plunged into the world of trees, swamp, pool, animals, stones, having frequent fainting spells. He remembered overhearing a conversation between his father and a friend which shocked him back to reality. His father had said: "What will become of the boy if he cannot earn his own living?"[6] From that time on he left his dalliance with his unconscious realm and became more conscientious than ever before, not for the sake of appearance but "so that I might amount to something, but for my own sake."[7] Looking back, he muses,

> That was when I learned what a neurosis is. . . . What led me astray during my crisis was my passion for being alone, my delight in solitude. . . . I immersed myself in nature, crawled as it were into the very essence of nature and away from the whole human world.[8]

The number two personality which Jung was so early aware of was close to nature, the earth, moon, and sun, the weather, all living creatures, especially close to night, to dreams and to "God." Grownup, old, mistrustful, "number two" was remote from the world of people. All through his childhood whenever he was alone he continued to seek the peace of this "other" personality, number two.

As it came time for him to go the university, he struggled with a choice of vocation. At this time he had a dream in which he held a tiny wind-threatened light cupped in his hands. On waking, he knew that the light was his consciousness, the only light he had. He now knew that his number one personality was the bearer of the light and that number two followed him like a shadow.

> In the role of Number one, I had to go forward, into studying, moneymaking, responsibilities, entanglements, confusions, errors, submissions, defeats, The storm pushing against me was time, ceaselessly flowing into the past, which just as ceaselessly dogs our heels. It exerts a mighty suction which greedily draws everything living into itself; we can only escape from it—for a while—by pressing forward. . . . I must leave Number two behind me, that was clear. But under no circumstances, ought I to deny him to myself or declare him invalid. . . . For there was no doubt in my mind that Number two had something to do with the creation of dreams and I could easily credit him with the necessary superior intelligence.[9]

This numinous experience of the Above and Below of his early four year old dream, this seductive realm which interfered with the ego development of the twelve year old boy, this ongoing experience of an archaic, wiser personality who was involved in dream creation, were all defining for Jung his unconscious before he had ever heard the word "unconscious." One other childhood vision, for a time agonizingly blocked from conscious recognition, a vision of a cathedral-shattering Christian God, added yet another key element to Jung's evolving view of the unconscious. He realized that he had not invented what was for him a horrible image of the cathedral. He believed that the image had been forced on him and that he had been compelled with utmost cruelty to think it. After he finally gave in and allowed the image into his conscious, he said that "an inexpressible feeling of grace came to me."[10] He began here to know what he was only to be able to clarify years later as the objective facticity, the givenness of the unconscious psyche, and, further, that the renewal of the self flows from the unconscious, no matter how frightening the elements that dwell there.

Jung studied medicine and then decided on psychiatry as his direction. In 1900 he had just begun his career as assistant in a psychiatric clinic in Zurich. He was asked by his chief, Professor Bleuler, to review Sigmund Freud's book about dream interpretation. He was impressed by much of what Freud had written. Freud worked on the assumption that dreams were not a matter of chance but were associated with conscious thought and problems. At this time Jung's burning question was about what actually takes place in the minds of the mentally ill. He soon wondered why the doctors did not listen to what the individual patients had to say, why their fantasies, dreams, and hallucinations were ignored, why their individuality was ignored.

Freud had initiated the empirical study of the unconscious mind in the 1890's; thus to him is attributed the discovery of the unconscious. Jung, like most others in the field, had been acquainted with Freud's work, although academic predjudice against Freud confined discussion of his theories to the corridors at psychiatric congresses and never let it reach the floor. By 1905, Jung's studies had led to his discovery through word association experiments of an element in the unconscious that he called a "complex." His work, he realized, supported Freud's theories, and however unpopular or damaging to himself academically, he felt impelled, again by his "Number two personality," to mention Freud in the publication of the results of his experiments. In 1906 he sent Freud a copy of his research results and in 1907 of his book, *The Psychology of Dementia Praecox.*

Their association went on until their break in 1913. In 1909, the two were together for seven weeks on a trip to Clark University in Worcester, Massachusetts to deliver lectures in America on Freud's movement of psychoanalysis. It was Freud's long awaited international recognition. During this intimate daily contact they analyzed each other's dreams. According to Jones, Freud's biographer, the theme of Freud's dreams was his concern and anxiety over the future of "his children" and their psychoanalytic movement.[11] Jung's account has himself, like a son, at thirty-four, following in his mature fifty-three year old leader's footsteps. Earlier in 1909, Freud had, under protest from his several older Jewish followers, named the Gentile Jung as his successor and "crown prince." Freud, feeling anti-Semitic restrictions, saw that a non-Jewish friend and colleague, especially one of the already somewhat distinguished stature of Jung, would help him become acceptable in the non-Jewish scientific community.

Jung, during this period of daily association, became upset however, when Freud would not supply personal associations to a dream because it was bad for his authority. Jung in retrospect saw that in that moment the end of their relationship was foreshadowed. This authority, "doctrine" tendency in Freud already disturbed him.

Following this, Jung told Freud a very important dream that Freud could not interpret. It was a very important dream in that, looking at it even now, it seems to be a symbolic expression of Jung's explorations of the psyche, especially the unconscious. Jung later said that his associations with it would have been a stage by stage description of his history to that time. The dream seems thus to be an amazing representation of Jung's conscious and unconscious, past, present and future. It foreshadowed the very differing psychology of the unconscious which would bring about his total break with Freud. As the dream speaks about level beneath level, deeper and deeper levels of Jung's house, Jung was to propose an unconscious with levels that went far deeper and wider than Freud ever imagined.

This was the dream as Jung himself recounts it in his autobiography:

> I was in a house I did not know, which had two stories. It was "my house." I found myself in the upper story, where there was a kind of salon furnished with fine old pieces in rococo style. On the walls hung a number of precious old paintings. I wondered that this should be my house, and thought, "not bad." But then it occurred to me that I did not know what the lower floor looked like. Descending the stairs, I reached the ground floor. There everything was much older, and I realized that this part of the house must date from about the fifteenth or sixteenth century. The furnishings were medieval; the floors were red brick. Everywhere it was rather dark. I went from one room to another, thinking, "Now I really must explore the whole house." I came upon a heavy door, and opened it. Beyond it, I discovered a stone stairway that led down into the cellar. Descending again, I found myself in a beautifully vaulted room which looked exceedingly ancient. Examining the walls, I discovered layers of brick among the ordinary stone blocks and chips of brick in the mortar. As soon as I saw this I knew that the walls dated from Roman times. My interest by now was intense. I looked more closely at the floor. It was of stone slabs, and in one of these I discovered a ring. When I pulled it the stone slab lifted, and again I saw a stairway of narrow stone steps leading down into the

> depths. These too I descended, and entered a low cave cut into the rock. Thick dust lay on the floor and in the dust were scattered bones and broken pottery like remains of a primitive culture. I discovered two human skulls, obviously very old and half-disintegrated. Then I awoke.[12]

Freud in attempting to analyze the dream asked for personal associations, not with the house or its levels, but specifically "a wish" in connection with the two skulls. Jung knew that Freud was driving at an unconscious "death wish" concealed in the dream. He violently resisted such an interpretation. Freud had the idea already that Jung wished for his early death as a father figure. Jung had his own intimations but, not trusting himself, told himself that he wanted Freud's opinion. So, unable to risk his own interpretation in the face of Freud's doctrinal interpretation of dreams as censoring unacceptable wishes, Jung lied. The death wish, he told Freud, could be toward his wife and sister-in-law. He felt the gulf between their mental worlds. Freud seemed relieved, Jung comments.

> I saw from this that he was completely helpless in dealing with certain kinds of dreams and had to take refuge in his doctrine. I realized that it was up to me to find out the real meaning of the dream.[13]

In his last essay, written shortly before his death, Jung refers to this same interaction with Freud again and says that right then he had an intuition about the role that the subjective factor plays in psychological understanding.

> My intuition consisted of the sudden and most unexpected insight into the fact that my dream meant *myself, my life, my world my whole reality* against a theoretical structure erected by another, strange mind for reasons and purposes of its own. It was not Freud's dream; it was mine, and I understood suddenly in a flash what my dream meant.[14]

It became a passion of Jung to allow his patients the freedom to interpret the symbolic language of their own unconscious which he believed sought to *reveal* itself, especially in dreams, and *not,* as Freud thought, censor, distort or conceal. He was turning Freud's theory upside down. The unconscious was a womb of new birth, new insight rather than merely a cesspool of repressed material of one's past.

It is possible and profitable to analyze this whole dream interaction from a Freudian perspective on Jung's unconscious remembering that Jung agreed with much of Freud's theory at that time and continued to do so, and indeed to build on it. He always said that there were some persons for whom a Freudian analysis was the correct one, though denying Freud's universal psychosexual emphasis, and his doctrinal restrictive view of the unconscious. While many personality theorists broke with Freud or criticized him for having too much emphasis on the unconscious and too little on the Ego, consciousness, and will, Jung stands alone in breaking with him because he saw Freud's emphasis on the unconscious as being not great enough!

Freudian analysis of Jung's unconscious at the time of this American trip dream would be a personal dynamic interpretation. In the context of his relationship with Freud, Jung's dream is colored by an unconscious inferiority. He says he didn't "trust" his own interpretations. There is "fear" in his resistance to Freud's interpretation and yet final submission to Freud's wishes. Was this fear of the father or of homosexual wishes? He says he didn't have any death wishes. Was this unconscious denial? He wouldn't present his views. Was this unconscious projection of all-powerful authority or a projection of his own aggression? Fearing loss of Freud's friendship, was this idealization or insecurity? Not "being up to" quarreling with Freud, was this fear of power? Lying, saying it was because he wanted Freud's thoughts, was this rationalization? Claiming that Freud was incapable of understanding Jung's mental world, could this be inflation as a defense to alleviate guilt about keeping his thoughts secret from this father figure? Was Freud not really Jung's

> ideal father since the relationship with his real father had always been unsatisfactory and his relationship with his mother had always been more satisfying? Did the skulls not then represent Jung's wish for the death of Freud?[15]

Shot through as these interpretations are with Freudian Oedipus theory and other elements of his "doctrine," they certainly seem to point to some accurate dimensions of Jung's personal psychology.

Jung apparently considered Freud a father figure. He once wrote a letter to Freud.

> I was overjoyed by your letter, being, as you know, very receptive to any recognition the father sees fit to bestow.[16]

Freud was committed to the rationalistic scientific point of view. He felt that only this would be accepted in a true scientific psychology. Anything that smacked of religion or the mystical, he saw as invalid and explainable on other reductive grounds. He assumed Jews in general more capable of this enlightened scientific approach, thus ignoring Jewish mystical tradition in Chassidism and Kabbala. He thus saw the unconscious as something to be programmed within the frame of predictability. He saw the unconscious processes clearly explained within his biologically connected theoretical framework. Thus he approached Jung's dream with a need for clear-cut interpretation concerning death wishes. The unconscious for him was regression, a product of repression. It corresponds roughly to what Jung was later to call the Shadow. The Shadow Jung saw to be a part of the unconscious, the gateway between the levels of the unconscious which he was to call the personal and collective unconscious. This shadow level of the unconscious was a constitutent of ego development. It is a "product" which comes about through the establishing of a center of awareness. It is that which we have measured and found wanting.

Freud, starting from symptoms of neurosis, made a good case for dreams as mediators of unconscious contents. He used free association moving out from dream images.

> What he elicited as contents of the unconscious seemed, on the face of it, to consist of elements that were quite capable of consciousness and had therefore been conscious under other conditions.[17]

To him they seemed to have been repressed because of their morally incompatible nature. They had been conscious and had become subliminal, more or less irrecoverable because of the counter-effects exerted by the conscious. The recovery of lost contents could happen if one let go and allowed oneself to be guided by association.

> This initial discovery logically led to the interpretation of the unconscious as a phenomenon of repression which could be understood in personalistic terms. . . . Freud later acknowledged the continued existence of archaic vestiges in the form of primitive modes of functioning, though even these were explained personalistically. On this view the unconscious psyche appears as a subliminal appendix to the conscious mind.[18]

Jung was to go beyond personalistic views of the unconscious. The first dream of the little boy which involved him with images so far beyond those of which he was personally capable, the historical levels beneath the first floor of "his house," all pointed to a more than personal unconscious. He was to spend the second half of his life verifying this theory factually. And while he saw the conscious as the tip of the iceberg and the unconscious as the greater submerged part, that part was not coextensive with personal history and biology. Jung's unconscious was to be a universe that reached back to the mysterious beginnings of time and forward infinitely. The personal, of course, had its importance; Jung was to define the personal unconscious as

> everything of which I know, but of which I am not at the moment thinking; everything of which I was once conscious but have now forgotten; everything perceived by my senses, but not noted by my conscious mind; everything which involuntarily and without paying attention to it I feel, think, remember, want, do, all the future things that are taking shape in me and will sometime come to consciousness, all this is the content of the unconscious. . . . To this marginal phenomenon which is born of alternating shades of light and darkness there also belong Freud's findings.[19]

In everyday life we have many examples of what Jung calls the personal unconscious. That forgotten ideas have not ceased to exist but are present in a subliminal state and can rise again spontaneously after many years of oblivion can be seen in every life. A person can be engaged in deep conversation and suddenly notice that her flow of thoughts has been interrupted by childhood memories. Seeking the cause, one may hear a child's street game or become aware of an odor that is associated with childhood. Having noticed the smell or heard the sound subliminally, the unconscious perception had been subliminal because the attention had been elsewhere engaged and the stimulus was not strong enough to deflect it and reach consciousness directly.

Something like a genuine but unrealized recollection is another example of personal unconscious functioning. One may be rereading a book one hasn't read in years and find there, almost word for word, sentences one has recently written, thinking all the while that the thought was original.

One may dream of oneself being ill and in a wheelchair and find oneself in a similar situation a few months later. The unconscious seems to know what is taking shape and will come to consciousness eventually.

A case of repression may be seen in someone of whom you are jealous being consistently "forgotten" in delivering mail or in introductions and acknowledgements. One may repress one's dishonesty, self-centeredness or lust and project it on another or on another race.

Such are the kinds of subliminal material, contents of the personal unconscious from which the symbols of our dreams may be spontaneously produced.

> This subliminal material can consist of all urges, impluses and intentions: all perceptions and intuitions, all rational or irrational thoughts, conclusions, inductions, and premises and all variety of feeling. Any or all of these can take the form of partial, temporary or constant unconscious.[20]

II. Farther into the Unconscious

In time Jung was to see and say that the unconscious was no mere depository of the past but the very matrix of consciousness, the womb of future psychic situations and ideas. He saw the unconscious as the source of creativity. How could sudden inspirations or the never before known answers to problems, even scientific discoveries which originate in dreams, be explained solely on the basis of memory?

He began to see consciousness more and more as a tiny island floating on the great sea of unconsciousness. He was aware of how fragile an acquisition consciousness was, how easily disassociations could occur. We can lose our identity. From moods, possessions, obsessions to psychosis, we see our vulnerability. Consciousness is a recent acquisition in the history of the race. Primitives, for example, may assume that they have a "bush soul." They believe that a certain tree or animal is an incarnation of a part of their soul. This dual soul concept shows how fragile is the unity and continuity of consciousness. It is this fear of being engulfed again by unconsciousness that Jung saw present in much resistance he met to his ideas, indeed to some people's even admitting the existence of an unconscious.

This was especially true when he began to say that the unconscious was more than personal. Beneath the layer of the personal appeared to be a deeper layer on which the personal unconscious rests. That deeper layer does not derive from personal experience but is inborn. The collective unconscious contains the whole spiritual heritage of humanity's evolution born anew in the brain structure of every individual.

> The collective unconscious includes contents resulting from the inherited possibilities of psychical functioning in general, namely from the inherited brain structure.[21]

Jung first chose the name "collective unconscious" because this part was not merely individual but universal.

> It has contents and modes of behavior that are similar everywhere and in all individuals. It is, in other words, identical in all men and thus constitutes a common psychic substrate of a super personal nature which is present in every one of us.[22]

Jung saw no reason why, if we take comparative anatomy seriously, we should not take the history of the psyche as seriously. This became his life's work. He engaged in painstaking research into the past, and as he did so this concept of the collective unconscious or objective psyche, as he later called it, grew. He began to reach the very subsoil of life itself, not only its instinctive sources but its spiritual ferment and essence as well. In this unconscious he found the

> deposit of mankind's typical reactions since primordial times to universal human situations such as love, birth, death, fear, danger, the struggle against superior powers, relations between the sexes, child and parent; hate and love, the power of the light or the dark principle.[23]

Jung tells of the practical use, as well as the confirmation, his theories had in many stories of modern patients. One very rational patient felt he was going insane. He recounted some of his experiences and a very impressive dream on his first visit to Jung. Going to his bookshelf, Jung showed him, in a four hundred year old book, a woodcut that was an almost exact, literal representation of the man's dream. His relief was enormous, as Jung said:

> You see, your dream is no secret. You are not shocked by a pathological insult and separated from mankind by an inexplicable psychosis. You are merely ignorant of certain experiences well within human knowledge and understanding.[24]

He pored over esoteric works of history to find more and more support for his theories.

> The psyche is not only of today. It reaches right back to prehistoric ages. Has man really changed in ten thousand years? . . . Of course the hairy man of the Ice ages has become unrecognizable when you try to discover him among the persons you meet on Fifth Avenue. But you will be amazed when you have talked to such moderns for hundreds of hours about their intimate life. You will then read the mouldy parchments as if they were the most recent thrillers. You will find the secrets of the modern consulting room curiously expressed in abbreviated Medieval Latin or by an intricate Byzantine hand.[25]

It was in these same worldwide and century after century repetitions of the same themes not only in historical records but in myths, fairytales, dreams, rites and works of art of all kinds that Jung began to see the universal symbolic communications of the objective psyche. The language here was a symbolic one, just as it had been back before the turn of the century when Freud and Josef Breuer had first inferred the unconscious when they recognized that neurotic symptoms could be symbolically meaningful. A paralysis may be saying symbolically that a person "can't go on anymore," or a spasm whenever a person tries to swallow may express that she "can't swallow" something in her life.

Jung had long been aware of the symbolic language of dreams and the need to find the personal associations with each symbol in the dream in order to determine what the dreamer's unconscious was trying to tell her. He believed that dreams should always be approached as meaningful and as being compensatory. They were the unconscious compensating for, or warning the conscious about, a direction it was taking. He felt that in our civilized life we have stripped so many ideas of their emotional energy that we hardly respond to them at all. Dreams can compensate. Their wealth of imagery can light up an idea and bring it home to us with great emotional impact so that we change our attitude and behavior. Dreams can connect us with healthy instincts, nature and truth, even according to Jung, with the most profound wisdom and truth of humanity and our own being.

The unconscious began to take on heights and depths never dreamed of, and it was a fact, an objective reality as real as the outer world on which our rational, scientific age had placed so much value. Jung did not want to denigrate or lose the accomplishments of the rationalistic, scientific West, but to have us integrate into our lives the irrational and more than rational, the intuitive, the instinctive, the soul. He perceived a dangerous separation of consciousness from the unconscious and especially from the collective unconscious. In our attempts to explain everything rationally, whole areas of human experience were being denied and rejected. History, but not exclusively the rational history of the West, and anthropology were links with what was being ignored.

The unconscious is the reality of the more than rational. However, Jung saw that the unconscious needed the conscious, the Ego, to give it flesh, and make it operative in the world. The conscious,

Jung saw as both inner and outer directed, introverted, and extraverted. It was more than thinking; it made its judgments by feeling or evaluation also, and it perceived by both sensing (using the senses) and intuition. Whichever one of each of these a person develops, so that the conscious personality is characterized by them, the opposites are undeveloped and so unconscious. In the second half of life a person needs to integrate the unconscious attitude and functions into the personality. The conscious needs, from the beginning of life, to integrate more and more of the unconscious and make it conscious, but it can never make conscious the whole contents of either the personal or the collective unconscious. Its attitude before the unconscious seems to be one of awe, since it is such a given. The unconscious is not only personal, it is transpersonal. It connects one to the more than "I."

Psyche, according to Jung, is not "tabula rasa" at birth. There is a given, a transpersonal built in. Like the body's instincts, the unconscious psyche has its inborn, pre-established patterns. Like a certain bird building a specific type of nest from an inherited inbuilt archetectural design, human beings too operate out of universal inbuilt unconscious archetypes. The bird uses the materials available in its outer environment. From the outer world of our environment, we put together our ways of living and relating: the flesh, fabric and colors of our myths, dreams, homes, rites, our hardware and software. Yet, there are certain detectable, repeated, established patterns that we follow.

> You see, we are born into a pattern, we are a pattern. We are a structure that is pre-established through the genes. It is a biological order of our mental functioning as, for instance, our biological, physiological function follows a pattern. The behavior of any bird or insect follows a pattern and that is the same with us. Man has a certain pattern that makes him specifically human and no man is born without it. We are only deeply unconscious of these facts because we live by our senses and outside of ourselves. If a man could look into himself, he could discover it.[26]

Jung saw the inbuilt patterns of the collective unconscious as operating everywhere. He spent years studying these archetypes of human behavior. He saw persons relating as Father, as Mother, as

Child. He saw the Father pattern operative within women and even children as well as in biological fathers. There is a typical, or ideal Father and we all know instinctively how to play the role. There is the Mother too and the Great Mother. The human selfless nurturing role can be assumed by any of us. There is the Great Mother, the source of life and fertility, of new life, renewal, rebirth. Mother Nature plays that role, Mother Earth plays it. A nation, a church, a movement, a queen or president can play it. The Mother or Great Mother can be all devouring and consuming as well as life supporting and renewing; she can be jealous, demanding devotion as well as giving care.

The Hero Archetype can be seen in poems and plays, movies, soap opera, history books and scriptures, paintings and statues, the television news and morning newspaper as well as in oneself and the woman or man next door. We all recognize and stir, however briefly, to the hero. Our emotional involvement is born of that commonality in our unconscious, our collectively shared unconscious potential which allows us to identify with and thrill to any heroic action.

There are archetypes of power—panic, violence, incest. These behaviors take different forms in different centuries and places but they seem nonetheless to be inbuilt patterns that are acted out. Jung gives an example of the behaviors (often violence and ambush) connected even from primitive times with the ford of a river. He calls it the archetype of the ford. He tells the story of a Swiss king, Albrecht, who was assassinated at a ford. His murderers had been following him for hours and could not come to consensus about whether to kill the king. The moment the king rode into the ford they were seized; this was the "right" moment and he was killed.

Jung's idea of being "seized by" an archetype he sees played out in cases of love at first sight. Here one is seized by the Anima or Animus: the feminine in man or the masculine in woman. These powerful archetypes have both positive and negative potential. The Ego development of the first half of life calls for the repression of the one or the other in order that a strong sense of femininity or masculinity can be achieved. In the second half of life, the man can be overcome by the negative Anima, in moodiness or in making poisonous, devaluing remarks, unless and until the positive characteristics culturally attributed to the opposite sex can be integrated and played out in his personality. The Anima can be met in the threatening guise of the "femme fatale" (a character often played out in drama or in life), in erotic fantasies, or she can be the guiding spirit and mediator of the inner world. She seems to grow more helpful in the process of encounter and polite interaction. Dreams and images taken seriously and lived seem to produce better and more helpful dreams and images. The Anima or any dream or unconscious figure becomes more real within the receptive person than in those who neglect their unconscious messengers and messages.

The Animus too can possess one in a negative way so that only afterward does one realize with horror that one has said and done things diametrically opposed to what one honestly thinks and feels. In dreams and in myths the negative animus is met by the woman as the death demon. Psychologically, he represents something that lures woman away from all human relationships, especially from contacts with real men. He presents a fantasy world of how things "ought to be." The negative animus is that part of the woman herself that can take the guise of a robber or murderer in dreams and be self-destructive, or other-destructive, coldness. Brutality, recklessness, empty talk, and silent obstinate evil ideas are all negative Animus characteristics.

But like the Anima, the Animus too has a positive and valuable side. The Beauty and the Beast motif tells of the transformation that occurs when Beauty loves and embraces the Beast. Kissed, the inner companion can open up initiative, courage, objectivity and spiritual wisdom.

> The Animus, just like the Anima, exhibits four stages of development. He appears first as a personification of mere physical power. . . . In the next stage he possesses initiative and capacity for planned action. In the third phase the animus becomes the "word," often appearing as a professor or clergyman. Finally, in the fourth manifestation, the Animus is the incarnation of "meaning." On the highest level he becomes (like the Anima) a mediator of religious experience whereby life acquires new meaning. He gives the woman spiritual firmness, an invisible inner support that compensates for her outer softness.[27]

A woman connected to this part of her own unconscious, her Animus, can be in touch with the spirit of the times to such a degree that she becomes extremely creative. She can be more and more receptive to bold creative ideas.

In Eastern thought, the energies of Yin and Yang are archetypal patterns which could perhaps subsume the so-called Anima, Animus and move the archetype beyond the present culturally patriarchial phase. In any case, another archetype which subsumes all the archetypes, the archetype of archetypes, is the Self. Like the turn of a kaleidoscope the unconscious of an individual presents its dominant characters one by one. Clear-cut distinctions and strict formulations of archetypes are impossible.

> A kind of fluid interpenetration belongs to the very nature of all archetypes. . . . No archetype can be reduced to a simple formula. It is a vessel which we can never empty and never fill. It has partial existence only, and when it takes shape in matter it is no longer what it was.[28]

Archetypes persist throughout the ages and demand ongoing reinterpreting. The best attempts at explanation are only approximate translations into another metaphorical language. The most we can do is give it modern dress. But whatever we do to it in interpretation, we do to ourselves, to an organ of our own psyche. A bad explanation means a bad and injurious attitude toward that psychic organ, a flawed connection between an archetype of our own unconscious and our conscious ego. Archetypes personify the roots of consciousness. The basic importance of the connection with these roots is seen in the constant concern and preoccupation for the "magic reality" of primitives and the "religio" or "linking back" of all religious life. There is no rational substitute for an archetype any more than there is a substitute for any human organ. "It is a well nigh hopeless undertaking to tear a single archetype out of the living tissue of the psyche."[29]

Neither can one tear the concept of archetype from that of the unconscious, personal and collective. Nor can one become involved in the history of myths and rites and the universal manifestations of archetypes of the unconscious and lose sight of the importance of maintaining and enhancing and enlarging the connections with consciousness. Everything is for connection, integration and wholeness. Jung's psychology is teleological. There is a built-in end or goal of personality. Each personality is tending, hungering, longing to become its own true Self. Individuation is what the personality is for. The archetype of the Self is the central core around which the personality unites, the union of conscious and unconscious. The Self is there in the Beginning and in the End. It is the Self that connects me beyond myself. Each of us and all of us are for humanity. The symbol of this is the Cosmic Man. In Christianity the Christ is the Cosmic Man, the Alpha and the Omega. His is the Wholeness of Humanity, the Divine living humanly. Each of us is called to the fullness of our own individual humanity as Christ lived the fullness of his humanity. "I have come," he said, "that you may have life and have it to the full."[30] In living this life of fullness each of us is to realize our true humanity and uniqueness.

The Archetype of the Self should bring us to true humanity, but it too can have its dark as well as light aspect if its integration is not truly human.

> The dark side of the Self is the most dangerous thing of all, precisely because the Self is the greatest power in the psyche. It can cause people to spin megalomaniac or self-delusory fantasies that catch them up and "possess" them. A person in this state thinks with mounting excitement that he has grasped and solved the great cosmic riddles; he therefore loses all touch with human reality.[31]

A constant danger for Christianity is that the Christ of faith will become a myth that is divorced from the historical Jesus of Nazareth. Myths and archetypes must maintain their connection to the psyche which gives them life as the psyche must maintain its connection (its "bending back") with the numinosity of myths and archetypes and each individual must maintain connection with our common clay.

The inner center, the true Self which personifies the Unconscious and draws consciousness to it like a magnet, is realized in a beautiful form by the Naskapi Indians who still exist in the forests of the Labrador peninsula. These hunting people live in isolated family groups far from one another and have never evolved tribal customs, collective religious beliefs or rituals. In solitude each person relies only on his or her inner voices and unconscious revelations. In their basic view of life, the soul is simply an "inner companion" whom he or she calls "my friend" or *mista peo. Mista peo,* the Great Man, dwells in the heart and is immortal; in the moment of death he leaves the individual and later reincarnates himself in another being.

These Naskapi, paying attention to their dreams and testing their truth, enter into deeper connection with the Great Man. The major moral imperative is thus to follow the instructions given in dreams and give concrete form to them in art. Lies and dishonesty drive the Great Man away, whereas love of one's neighbor and generosity attract him and give him life. Dreams give each one directions as to his or her way in the inner world and in the outer world. They help foretell weather and aid in hunting. Such is the harmony of individuation, the wedding of the conscious and unconscious. With Jung each such person might say, "My life is the self-realization of the unconscious."

Notes

1. C.G. Jung, *Memories, Dreams, Reflections,* recorded and edited by Aniela Jaffe, translated by Richard and Clara Winston (New York: Vantage Books, 1965) p. 3.
2. *Ibid.*, p. 5.
3. John Freeman, "Introduction," *Man and His Symbols,* edited by C.G. Jung and M.L. Von Franz (New York: Doubleday, Windfall Books, 1964) p. 12.
4. C.G. Jung, *Memories, Dreams, Reflections,* p. 15.
5. *Ibid.*, p. 30.
6. *Ibid.*,p. 31.
7. *Ibid.*
8. *Ibid.*, p. 32.
9. *Ibid.*, pp. 88–89.
10. *Ibid.*, p. 62.
11. Earnest Jones, *The Life and Work of Sigmund Freud* (New York: Basic Books 1955), pp. 11, 53–62.
12. C.G. Jung, *Memories, Dreams, Reflections,* pp. 158–159.
13. *Ibid.*, p. 160.
14. C.G. Jung, "Approaching the Unconscious," *Man and His Symbols,* edited by C.G. Jung, p. 57.

15. C. Jess Groesbeck, "The Analyst's Myth: Freud and Jung as Each Other's Analyst," *Quadrant,* Spring 1980, pp. 33–36.

16. C.G. Jung, *The Freud/Jung Letters,* edited by W. McGuire (New Jersey: Princton University Press, 1974), as quoted by Duane Schultz, *Theories of Personality* (Monterey, California: Brooks/Cole Wadsworth Co., 1976), p. 121.

17. C.G. Jung, *On the Nature of the Psyche,* translated by R.F.C. Hull (New Jersey: Princeton University Press, Bollingen Series, 1960), p. 89.

18. *Ibid.*, p. 89.

19. *Ibid.*, p. 95.

20. C.G. Jung, "Approaching the Unconscious," *Man and His Symbols,* p. 37.

21. C.G. Jung, *Psychological Types. A Theory of Individuation*, translated by R.F.C. Hull (New Jersey: Princeton University Press, Bollingen, 1971), p. 485.

22. C.G. Jung, *The Archetypes and the Collective Unconscious,* translated by R.F.C. Hull (New Jersey: Princeton University Press, Bollingen, 1959), p. 4.

23. Jolanda Jacobe, *The Psychology of C.G. Jung* (New Haven: Yale University Press, 1962), p. 10.

24. C.G. Jung, "Preface," *Psyche and Symbol,* edited by Violet S. de Laszlo (New York: Doubleday, Anchor, 1958), p. xv.

25. *Ibid.*, pp. xiii–xiv.

26. C.G. Jung, *Jung on Elementary Psychology. A Discussion Between C.G. Jung and Richard I. Evans* (New York: E.P. Dutton Co., 1976), p. 72.

27. M.L. von Franz, "The Process of Individuation," *Man and His Symbols,* edited by C.G. Jung and M.L. von Franz (New York: Doubleday, 1964), p. 194.

28. C.G. Jung, "The Psychology of the Child Archetype," *The Archetypes and the Collective Unconscious,* translated by R.F.C. Hull (New Jersey: Princeton University Press, Bollingen, 1959), p. 179.

29. *Ibid.*

30. Jn 10:10.

31. M.L. von Franz, "The Process of Individuation," p. 190.

CHAPTER 3

Prayer and the Unconscious in the Second Half of Life

I. Experiencing the Unconscious

The human being, intricate and amazing, begins life floating in an inner sea. The womb, our first environment, creates a dark, cushioned space for the ever-expanding, water-filled sac in which we grow to birth. Each of us begins our genetically-coded story in this place of unconsciousness. In this state, we know in our unconsciousness a profound connection with the universe and the history of the evolution of humanity as a product of the universe. This kind of knowing is primal. Its traces stay with us always, even after, as children of the twentieth century, we reduce the word "knowing" to point only to the achievement of rational scientific consciousness of which we are so proud.

What is this other way of knowing that we, from our evolutionary perspective, would call unknowing, this knowledge that we picture as having been eaten up, blotted out, by the developing consciousness of the human child or of the human race? The same twentieth century science has rediscovered this way of our being and knowing, has empirically observed its behavior and named it the unconscious. But we still resist this aspect of ourselves. Whole schools of modern psychology still deny the existence of an unconscious. Other schools limit its significance and insist on concentrating attention on the conscious.

There is no doubt a profound rightness about this insistence on the study of human consciousness and human behavior. We are rightly proud of the achievements of human reason and human will. Modern technology is no mean accomplishment. Flying from one part of the globe to another, talking to one another and seeing images of one another across the world has expanded our horizons. The very discovery of being on a planet traveling around a star has changed our self-image, increased our truth, stretched our reason. The efforts to move off the earth on to our satellite and create satellites from which to do our work of observing, recording, beaming has expanded human productivity and will. The information explosion of the computer age and the control we have achieved over the resources of the earth have made us more conscious beings as the consciousness of the universe. We have multiplied and magnified each of the human senses so that we have altered our perception of time and space, transformed our environment and even our own bodies.

In the process we have valued parts of ourselves and ways of being human that should be valued. Yet it is possible that we have devalued and cast off parts of ourselves and ways of being human that are genuine and also extremely valuable.

It seems from many indications that we are at a boundary. Our dissecting of the material things of our earth has led us back to symbolic thinking about invisible particles of matter, back from infinite progress to imagining a shockingly possible cataclysmic outcome of the whole human enterprise. We have been brought face to face with our limitations by recognizing the pollution of our atmosphere that has been the by-product of our progress. We can see in our living rooms the human suffering and violence breeding impoverishment that is the by-product of first world wealth and technology. We can hold our breath again and again at the threat of nuclear annihilation from each new conflict over territorial sovereignty that springs up around the globe. We are turned back from making things and going places to look at ourselves. We need to study our own psyche, our motivations, our meanings. We recognize that we will be the authors of all coming evil. More than ever before we need to look inward and know ourselves. Assassination after assassination has shown us that any one of us is capable of affecting the destiny of nations, killing a symbol of hope. Assassin after assassin has been an example of conscious and unconscious gone awry.

Carl G. Jung was one of many twentieth century persons who was at pains to understand the workings of the human psyche. His perception was that modern humanity was sick because the human person today is not whole. We have lost touch, he believed, with the primitive and instinctive side of the personality in our all-out effort to advance progress. In losing touch with the unconscious we have lost touch with our roots, and also with a larger vision of humanity. He was not advocating the overthrow of consciousness but the ongoing process of each person's integrating more and more from the unconscious into consciousness. He saw human reason as being supplemented by what is known to the unconscious.

At the outbreak of the First World War he felt that people were still quite certain that the world could be righted by rational means but that "there are not a few people nowadays who are convinced that mere human reason is not entirely up to the enormous task of fettering the volcano."[1] He envisioned an ongoing relationship of the conscious with the vast sea of unconsciousness out of which it grew. For Jung the unconscious was a womb of creativity, not merely a dumping ground for contents too despicable or painful for consciousness to acknowledge. For him "the mind of a child grows out of the unconscious."[2] Yet he further states: "Psychology teaches us that, in a certain sense, there is nothing in the psyche that is old, nothing that can really definitively die away. . . . Whoever protects himself against what is new and strange and thereby regresses to the past falls into the same neurotic condition as the man who identifies himself with the new and runs away from the past. The only difference is that one has estranged himself from the past and the other from the future."[3]

In the past of each of us is the unconscious, not only what he called the personal unconscious, the product of individual subjective experience, but our inheritance of the unconscious. The growth of consciousness in the first half of life is the growth of ego. The child who at first in a primitive way begins to recognize persons and things as outside of herself begins finally to speak of herself in the first person. At the beginning of another stage of ego development (the adolescent transition), the young adult, moving out of the psychic womb of the early environment, encounters a welter of problems and conflicting values. She chooses among those offered ideals, convictions, attitudes, guiding ideas, and dreams and seems to become them, as attention is focused on achievements and usefulness and making her way in the world. The conscious seems to be identified with this Ego one is building up for some thirty-five to forty years. One is named primarily by the outside world in the adapting.

Again at mid-life a significant change in the human psyche seems to be in preparation. This time, however, the call to transformation comes from within. "At first, it is not a conscious and striking change; it is rather a matter of indirect signs of a change which seems to take its rise from the unconscious. Often it is something like a slow change in a person's character; in another case, certain traits may come to light which had disappeared in childhood; or again, inclinations and interests begin to weaken and others arise to take their place."[4] It is as though a second personality begins to emerge. The Ego has been the center. Jung, however, calls the true center of the psyche the Self. The Self now begins to replace the Ego as central. This archetype of archetypes embraces both the conscious and the unconscious personality. Individuation means becoming one's Self. This movement toward wholeness is the particular adventure of the second half of life. The flowering of the Self begins in the unconscious. The Self encompasses all the undeveloped potentials, all the unlived life, so now it is much more a life that flows from within, rather than a continuing adaptation to the outside world. Jung distinguishes between a psychology of life's morning and afternoon. The neuroses of the young are usually a shrinking away from the concrete ends, from Ego development, and in this sense, a shrinking back from life. The neuroses of older patients came mainly from clinging to an attitude which is now out of season, a holding on to the meanings, values and goals that were appropriate to the first half of life.

Jung sees the ideal of the second half of life as a development of an even higher consciousness, a fuller development of the psyche and of the personality. Yet he remarks: "Society does ot value these feats of the psyche very highly; its prizes are always given for achievement and not for personality—the latter being rewarded for the most part posthumously."[5] Because of this there are too few artists of life, too few who succeed in draining the whole cup of life with grace. Too many people continue in the second half of life to look outward, to compete with youth, to go on striving for possessions and achievements. The irony of personality being valued only *after* a person's life may point in a paradoxical way to a deeper truth about life that the religions of the world have long held, that is, the spark of divinity in each person and the survival of our personality after death. A large number of people have from time immemorial felt the need to believe in the continuance of life, and in death as a transition. For Jung, those live most fully and are most healthy who see death as a goal. He observed that the psyche in old people ignores the fact that it is apparently threatened with the complete end. It behaves as if it were going on. Thus, living in the second half of life as though one had centuries was his advice.

Modern scientific thinking finds such a belief in the continuation of life unprovable, irrational, even infantile. It is one of the many such religious beliefs that need to be outgrown in the modern era. To these modern denials Jung offers his insights about the unconscious. He saw that through one's unconscious one might experience anew some of humanity's ancient truths. He invites each person to this kind of dialogue with the unconscious.

> Do we ever understand what we think? We only understand that thinking which is a mere equation and from which nothing comes out but what we have put in. That is the working of the intellect. But beyond that there is thinking in primordial images—in symbols which are older than historical man; which have been ingrained in him from earliest times and eternally living, outlasting all generations, still make up the groundwork of the human psyche. It is only possible to live the fullest life when we are in harmony with these symbols; wisdom is a return to them. It is neither a question of belief nor of knowledge, but of the agreement of our thinking with the primordial images of the unconscious. They are the source of all our conscious thoughts, and one of these primordial thoughts is the idea of life after death. Science and these symbols are incommensurables. They are indispensable conditions of the imagination; they are primary data—the materials whose expediency and warrant to exist science cannot deny offhand. It can only treat them as given facts much as it can explore a function like that of the thyroid gland, for example. Before the nineteenth century the thyroid was regarded as a meaningless organ, merely because it was not understood. It would be equally short-sighted of us today to call the primordial images senseless. For me these images are something like psychic organs, and I treat them with the very greatest care. It happens sometimes that I must say to an older patient: "Your picture of God or your idea of immortality is atrophied; consequently your psychic metabolism is out of gear." The ancient medicament of immortality is more meaningful than we supposed.[6]

How does one experience these inner facts, these psychic organs, this thinking in primordial images? How does one experience these ingrained and eternally living symbols, this groundwork of the human psyche? How can one be in harmony with these symbols? Whence comes the agreement of one's thinking with the primordial images of the unconscious, these sources of all our conscious thoughts, these indispensable conditions of the imagination, this primary data, this given? Jung encouraged attentiveness to dreams and to the images that arise spontaneously when conscious thinking is quieted. Such ways of quieting have also always been found in the prayer traditions of all religions. Presence to one's unconscious is a relating to the "there within one," to otherness. In this relating, this communing, the otherness takes the initiative. "First hand experiences of otherness are open to all of us, if we are open to the presence and communications of our unconscious. . . . There is no possibility of learning to live in long range commitment to otherness as an objective dimension of our lives articulated in religious belief if we initially choose to defend against all consciousness of the pulsating currents of the unconscious."[7]

It seems strange to speak of one's unconscious as other, and yet this is truly how we experience it. When one's unconscious "slips out" one produces an unintended effect. We are shocked when someone replies angrily to an innocent statement of ours like "Please pass the salt" with "You said that in a tone that implied I was torturing you by deliberately withholding the salt." The unconscious said more then we intended! In dreams and fantasy, ideas come that surprise us and often they are laden with authoritative, direction-giving emotional energy. One is incapable of producing these phenomena at will or of anticipating these contents.

In his observations of thousands of patients, Jung attested not only to the otherness of the unconscious but to its more than solely personal nature and to its religious significance. "I have to admit that the unconscious mind is capable at times of assuming an intelligence and purposiveness which are superior to actual conscious insight. There is hardly any doubt that this fact is a basic religious phenomenon."[8] For him the conscious personality was part of the whole, a small circle contained in a bigger one, the tip of the iceberg, "In other words, there is unavoidably an illimitable and indefinable addition to every personality."[9] For this reason practically each experience, object, fact contains something which is unknown. He saw reason as supplemented by intuition.

> My psychological experience has shown time and again that certain contents issue from a psyche more complete than consciousness. They often contain a superior analysis

> or insight or knowledge which consciousness has not been able to produce. We have a suitable word for such occurrences—intuition. In pronouncing it most people have an agreeable feeling as if something had been settled. But they never take into account the fact that they do not *make* an intuition. On the contrary, it always comes to you. You *have* a hunch, it has produced itself and you only catch it if you are clever or quick enough.[10]

In treating his patients Jung found himself supporting this wider personality, as he called it. He experienced the mysterious healing effects of such a course. "I always let him see that I was on the side of the (dream) voice which I recognized as part of his future greater personality destined to relieve him of his one-sidedneess."[11] Our unconscious seems to go before us and lead us. If we live life to the fullest, we live it in dynamic relationship with our unconscious. Our unconscious connects us to our past which also connects us to the universe. Subtle as it is, our unconscious connects us to the mystery of our true Self, opens us to another kind of knowing. "Nor can one unqualifiedly maintain that a Self which is not conscious cannot be known and is therefore no legitimate object of discussion. Although the unconscious, as such, undoubtedly escapes the direct glance of perceptive awareness, it may well manifest itself indirectly as the achievements of depth psychology have shown."[12]

II. Mystical Experience

The experience of the Self has always been found to be more than consciousness, exceeding the bounds of ego consciousness in sleep, trance, artistic creation, in daydreams and especially in the case of those who have reached for the most intense experiences of the Self—the mystics. The universal claims of the mystics seem to be describing the same inner world as the one explored by Jung. They too seem to be pointing to depths within, far deeper and wider than can ever be imagined. Jung explored the unconscious and happened on the human urge to the divine. Prayer has been the path of the mystics. It has made its contribution to their psychological wholeness, their individuation. "On their way to the love of God, mystics happen upon the graces of interiority—the largest of them a clear sense of presence, of things, of themselves, of other beings. Mystics come across and must meet directly with the power and life of psychic images, the repressed contents of their own personalities and their own particular culture."[13]

While psychic health cannot be simply identified with the sanctification of the soul, neither can we simply "erect physical or metaphysical boundaries between the realms of psyche and soul without a serious distortion of the reality of human experience and the risk of serious damage to both centers of our interior life."[14] So we can see that there have always been and are prayer forms which are both related to the unconscious and to the development of the true Self which is the particular goal of the second half of life. From this perspective prayer and the process of individuation have important mutual contributions to make to one another.

"The mystic's goal as manifested in his lifelong dedication to the absolute is to gradually expand his consciousness by moving more deeply into the 'inner world' of his personal feeling until its innermost depth is reached, what he usually refers to as the Self or God."[15] Yet for the true mystic the journey inward cannot be mere flight from the world, a collapsing of ego consciousness.

> The mystic's life may be seen as a recognition of the existence of the inner personal experiences which though independent of, and even antagonistic to, the social reality cannot be fully developed unless the individual also affirms his role in society. . . . What is needed is the integration of these inner experiences with the various social roles one adopts. The mystic provides the example of the method whereby the inner and outer may be joined; the schizophrenic, the tragic result when they are separated.[16]

The goal of Christian mysticism has never been the mystical experience in itself but the love of God, neighbor and self. Jesus spent whole nights in prayer and taught his disciples to pray, but in a rhythm of inner and outer activity all bathed in love. Peter cannot build his tent on the mount of the transfiguration and Jesus is called from prayer because he has "compassion on the multitude." There is always the call to integration, to action as well as to contemplation. "Though the mystic and scizophrenic ostensibly share the same flight from the social world the mystic's abandonment is merely of his own dependent attachments to it. Thus the mystic's life is in essence a process of freeing himself from those habits and customs that had been adopted as security measures to protect against the anxiety that inevitably accompanies any growth or movement toward independence."[17] The mystic moves toward a true freedom of spirit.

Prayer processes are processes of detachment and freedom; even prayers of petition that seem to be focused on conscious concerns are opening those concerns beyond the small circle of the ego to the Other. There are prayer forms that are an even more complete letting go in God of the concerns of one's everyday conscious ego. "The Spirit too helps us in our weakness, for we do not know how to pray as we ought; but the Spirit himself makes intercession for us with groanings which cannot be expressed in speech. He who searches hearts knows what the Spirit means, for the Spirit intercedes for the saints as God himself wills."[18]

The revelations of the Scriptures and of the mystics sound many common notes with Jung's description of the healthy person in the second half of life.

> It is highly important for a young person who is still unadapted and has as yet achieved nothing to shape the conscious ego as effectively as possible—that is, to educate the will. . . . It is otherwise with the person in the second half of life who no longer needs to educate his conscious will, but who, to understand the meaning of his individual life, must learn to experience his own inner being. Social usefulness is no longer an aim for him, although he does not question its desirability. Fully aware as he is of the social unimportance of his creative activity, he looks on it as a way of working out his own development and thus benefiting himself. These last achievements in turn serve to further the patient in his social existence. For an inwardly sound and self-confident person will be more adequate to his social tasks than one who is not on good terms with his unconscious.[19]

The explorations of these inner realms by the mystics give them another experience of reality which enriches their lives, as Jung's patients found in their intercourse with the unconscious. But the

Christian mystics are of one voice in pointing to the transcendence found in this realm:

> An altogether different layer of selfhood hides underneath the familiar succession of outward oriented phenomena. Behind the gates to this restricted area, the laws ruling ordinary consciousness seem to be suspended. Space and time recede or are transformed from a priori forms of outward perceptions into vistas of an inner realm with unknown rhythms and successions. From archaic depths the imagination (if it has not taken leave altogether) conjures well structured visions known to the dream consciousness only through fragments and to the waking consciousness not at all. In privileged instances the intellectual intuition, so preemptorily exorcized by Kant's critique, reasserts its rights and the mind literally perceives as directly as the senses. Does all this not support William James' observations that the ordinary rational consciousness is only one kind of consciousness, while all around it, separated from it by the flimsiest screens, there are potential forms of consciousness of a completely different nature? To James, the psychologist, the full knowledge of the self requires the contribution of the peak religious experiences.[20]

The full knowledge of the Self, in the overwhelming testimony of the mystics, includes a transcendent dimension. The Self participates actively in what we have come to call God. It is of and for God. The Self far surpasses the apparent boundaries of individual personhood. In Eckhart's daring expression: "There is something in the soul so closely akin to God that it is already one with him and need never be united to him. . . . If he were wholly this he would be both uncreated and unlike any creature."[21] Jan Ruusbroec, a Flemish mystic, consistently with great theological strength elaborated the same theme. "The soul is from all eternity an archetype within God. To the extent that its actual existence in time is essentially connected with this archetypical image, it 'dwells in God, flows forth from God, depends on God and returns to God'; the nobleness which the mind possesses by its very nature, it cannot lose without ceasing to exist altogether."[22]

Humanity can, it seems, experience itself in this transcendent way. There is an experience of this Beyond available to each member of the race and that experience is in modern psychological terminology experiencing in and through one's unconscious. Jung in his work with the unconscious came to have immense reverence for the religious dimension of the psyche. While he maintained the unknowability of God-in-himself, he came to assert that the Divine Image within the depths of the human was a real and observable fact. For him this experience of the activity and presence of the God image within could only be objectively examined and described as a psychological reality. Yet for him too, the universality of this psychological reality in the total experience of the human race points toward this immanent psychological reality's being the manifestation of a transcendent reality.

Belief in God is a real assent to a relationship. One's own inner self is in dynamic relationship with this ultimate Other. This Other who is completely unknowable to the human intellect, utterly beyond any concepts, has been known in a real and intimate way. Is this the knowing that is unknowing, the experience of knowing again what each of us was introduced to from our very origin, the experience of the unconscious? Is faith consciousness embracing these whispers from within as revelation of the Transcendent Other? Is it an appropriation of the archetype of the Self as a manifestation of God? William James seems to be referring to a knowing through the Unconscious when he discusses the noetic quality of the mystical experience. "Although so similar to states of feeling, mystical states seem to those who experience them to be also states of knowledge. They are states of insight into depths of truth unplumbed by the discursive intellect. They are illuminations, revelations, full of significance and importance all inarticulate though they remain; and as a rule they carry with them a curious sense of authority for aftertime."[23]

James Fowler seems to be pointing in the same direction when he calls faith a way of knowing.

> The kind of knowing or interpreting that faith is needs to be clarified further. Faith is that knowing or construing by which persons or communities recognize themselves as related to the ultimate conditions of their existence. In this sense faith is a knowing or construing which fixes on the relatedness of a person or a community to power(s), bound-

> aries (such as death or finitude), and source(s) of being, value and meaning which impinge on life in a manner not subject to personal control. In theological language, faith is the knowing or construing by which persons apprehend themselves as related to the Transcendent.[24]

In the psychology of the Scholastics on which their theology was based, there is nothing in the intellect that is not first in the senses. The knowledge that came to the *mystics* was, however, an exception to this! It was considered to be directly *infused* into the soul. In later spiritual theology the grace of infused contemplation was thought to be an extraordinary grace for an elite of specifically chosen people. Others might only aspire to acquired contemplation which was an "ordinary grace." Among modern theologians there is a questioning of this distinction. Karl Rahner is one who questions this: "Mysticism . . . occurs within the framework of normal graces and within the experience of faith."[25] The universal call to mysticism and to contemplation as the prayer path to this faith experience reflects this new understanding of faith as a way of experiencing rather than something added. Faith was imaged as something that *followed* knowledge and added to knowledge its own fine images of the universe. It was a vertical relationship to an unknowable and unimaginable God; it did not experience the world. A classical vocabulary was set up to make necessary distinctions which were historically necessary in order to maintain the transcendence of God. It "set up certain sharp but necessary distinctions between experience and faith, evidence and faith, imagination and faith."[26] Today this vocabulary and the enormous theological structure that went with it tends to be interpreted as maintaining not the transcendence of God, but the superfluousness of God. God has been pushed so far beyond human experience as to make no difference at all to human life.

The reversal of this is the understanding of faith and prayer as its expression, as a way of experiencing the world. Faith is then not "added to" but is "the most primary, the most elemental force in human nature; it is a force which *precedes* what we ordinarily call knowledge and all the forms of specific knowing; the force is uneducated and needs education; it is educated by knowledge of every kind, by people to every degree, by irony but not by every irony; last of all it is formed and educated by Christ."[27] This reverses the notion that faith is prefaced by rationality and brings us back to faith as underpinning rationality; back to what again resembles the unconscious which needs to be "educated" by the conscious.

These ideas which distinguish faith from the religious expressions of faith, however sublime those expressions, seem at the same time to democratize the experience of the mystics. Mysticism occurs, in Rahner's phrase, within the experience of faith. There is a vast body of experiential evidence of a spiritual experience which is known to the simplest as well as to the learned. It is expressed in Jung's "knowledge of a Divine Image," in the crudest expression of religious relationship in popular hymns about God or Jesus as *Friend,* as well as in the magnificent language of mystical poetry.

There is a "higher faculty," a form of consciousness, or is it perhaps unconsciousness, which receives that vast perpetual outpouring of the Power at the source of the universe as Divine Self-giving, the emmanation of an Infinite Lover into the ground of being of each of us. This is an experience which none of us completely captures, or contains, or exhausts. We do not experience this as our own, but as of Another, and at the same time we experience ourselves as needing to throw ourselves open to this inexhaustible Self-giving.

Bernard Lonergan calls this religious experience, religious conversion, falling in love unrestrictedly. He quotes Paul in Romans 5: We experience "the love of God poured forth in our hearts by the Holy Spirit who is given to us." We experience the divine initiative. It is an overwhelming seduction. When known thus as given, one has already opened oneself to the gift. This is prayer. This whole-person surrender which is, at the deepest center of the soul, profound activity is prayer. Whenever this incarnating of God in each person is affirmed, however subtly or overtly in a faithing person, praying is happening.

Psychologically speaking, Jung speaks of this kind of numinous experience as the human soul harboring a mystery which *means everything* to the one who has it. "One could even define religious experience as that kind of experience which is characterized by the highest appreciation, no matter what its contents are."[28] In case after case Jung saw the emergence of symbol of wholeness from the unconscious as having such a compelling quality and effecting a transforming influence on his patients. Time and again he saw this effect and attempted to understand why this kind of vision had such an effect upon the person. "The vision was a turning point in the patient's psychological development. It was what one would call in the language of religion a conversion."[29] His probing the history of these symbols led to their connection with ancient religious beliefs and the conclusion that the "unconscious mind has worked along the same lines of thought which has manifested itself time and again within the last two thousand years."[30] Jung saw in his work with people that these symbols are convincing to the modern mind however consciously skeptical or a-religious because they are simply overwhelming. And he summarizes: "If such experience helps to make your life healthier, more beautiful, more complete and more satisfactory to yourself and those you love, you may safely say: 'This was the grace of God.' "[31]

III. Prayer and Individuation

In Jung's work it was analysis that prepared the ground for the happening of such numinous experiences. In analysis the conscious personality was led into a more healthy and life-giving relationship with the unconscious personality. For Jung, most of his patients in the second half of life were in difficulty because of a loss of faith. Meaning was lost to them. Recovery of religious experience was the cure. In the history of Christianity prayer has been such a journey inward and an opening of the self to the experience of God. Prayer prepares the ground for the happening of religious experience. Prayer opens consciousness beyond itself, and this is true of the simplest petitionary prayer as well as of the unitive prayer of the mystic. In my cry to God, I move beyond my closed ego. Prayer is a way of overcoming the division between the conscious and the unconscious. "This is brought about by descending into that depth (or superconsciousness) in which is gathered up the totality of the spiritual experience of the human race."[32]

Prayer is another way of coming in touch with reality. It has its noetic quality. It gives us knowledge beyond the reach of rational thought. "Prayer implies and involves a passing over to the other. . . . Prayer is not a retreat from reality but rather a search for reality beyond the distortions of self-interest . . . a passing over to the divine standpoint, to the very limited extent that this is possible for man. In the very effort to pass over to the divine, however, man begins to transcend the ingrained relativities of his own very partial and partisan perception. From that journey he can only return home chastened and yet immensely enriched."[33] Prayer carries us to a vision of an inner relatedness to all things. As such, it is the source of an inner power. It generates in us an energy which is beyond the energy flow that is available in life, as we can lead it enclosed in everyday conscious activity. Prayer is activity beneath activity.

In the second half of life the Self begins to quicken. Gradually, the ego lets go its despotic hold to allow undeveloped parts of the personality to emerge from the unconscious and be integrated. Many people in the mid-life transition experience a listlessness, a stillness, a call to solitude, a need for inwardness. Deep within, in the midst of apparent non-activity, in the midst of this deadness a new birth, a resurrection, is in preparation. The way of conscious effort is giving way to the way of non-action. "The way of conscious effort is particularly important in the first part of life and in the pre-mystical stage. Quite simply it is the way of the person who thinks, asks questions, deliberates, weighs the evidence and makes decisions."[34] This way of decision builds one's life and affects the world around one. Through decisions one creates one's life style and builds one's character. If one is somewhat in touch with the Self and is unrestrictedly in love with God, one will perhaps pray and meditate according to the ways of conscious effort. "They will think about the Bible or they will make lengthy prayers to God with fervor and devotion or they will repeat the Jesus prayer with considerable effort and they will make resolutions to do good works."[35]

The way of non-action is more completely the way of the second half of life. Here one is less preoccupied with doing, with building up and tearing down, and is more into letting happen. Not that one is drifting and not making decisions—far from it—but one allows decisions to well up from inside. One waits on the truth that is deep within one's center. There is a great paradox involved in this seeming non-activity, for when the person now seems to be inactive a deeper force within is doing enormous things. One is allowing the creative power at one's center to emerge. The creative power at the center of the universe accomplishes in one what so much effort in life's morning could not yet accomplish. This is the great art of letting things happen. The prayer form that seems to be natural to this time is a prayer of recollection or the prayer of quiet. St. Teresa, as Donald Gelpi sees it in her description of the fourth mansion in the Interior Castle, her personal testimony about her own growth in prayer, corresponds to Jung's account of growth after the mid-life crisis. "In the fourth mansion conscious contact is re-established with the deeper aspects of the self. The despotic control of the rational ego begins to break down. There is newfound passivity in prayer. The heart of the God seeker becomes aware of a quiet center of recollected religious consciousness that is other than the busy ego, although the latter still bustles about like Martha with its images and abstractions. But ego awareness has ceased to be the primary locus of one's conscious relationship with God."[36] As passive openness intensifies, the ego is further calmed, and eventually absorbed into the prayer of quiet. Practically, this involves the abandonment of reasoning and thinking and of any effort. There is an intensification of loving openness to God.

This form of quiet prayer or loving and peaceful attentiveness to God with its disinclination to think about anything may seem to be laziness as one begins to be drawn to it. This seeming waste of time with nothing seeming to happen is the most profound happening. One is allowing oneself to be loved by God. When in empty faith I am doing nothing, a limitless divine love is welling up within me and taking over my life. The emptiness, the void, the darkness is infinite Love dwelling in the depths of my being.

One can experience this prayer of non-action before one reaches the second half of life, but when one has experienced the transition to that time when one's mortality and one's shadow has become a reality, non-action takes on a different aura. When one is still in the time of ego building, will and control are, and need to be, very important. In the afternoon of life one may still believe that one must work as if everything depended on oneself and pray as if everything depended on God, but one has definitely shifted the emphasis to the second part of the statement. One has experienced now the vast areas of one's lack of control. Having suffered life's losses, one knows the power of evil. One has gone through the end of naiveté and faced the threat of the void.

In the second half of life non-attachment takes on its own flavor. One is constantly now leaving what is familiar to enter on a terrain that is unfamiliar. One may remain in the same job and relationships but one will still be radically changed. Passing through ever new stages of the psyche, one will come to see things differently and feel the shift of values. "Take no gold or silver . . . nor a staff" (Mt 10:9–10). Letting go of anxiety, of discursive thinking, even of the joys of mystical consolations, noble thoughts or charismatic manifestations, one needs to be now in prayer as the "lilies of the field." One is led to unity with nature and the universe. Prayer can just simply be this kind of unity. One is passionately concerned for the poor and downtrodden. One is forgiving and has a compassion born of the experience of one's own weakness. One's prayer is altruistic. The tiniest leaf can kindle wonder and the sense of unity. All is in God and God is in all. The unconsciousness or the womb where one knew unity with the All is approached again but now with all the differentiation, all the plurality of life's experiences, all the richness of consciousness.

Notes

1. Carl G. Jung, *Psychology and Religion* (New Haven: Yale University Press, 1938), p. 59.
2. Carl G. Jung, "Stages of Life," *Modern Man in Search of a Soul,* translated by W. S. Dell and Cary F. Baynes (New York: Harcourt, Brace and World, 1933), p. 114.
3. *Ibid.*, p. 102.
4. *Ibid.*, p. 104.
5. *Ibid.*
6. *Ibid.*, pp. 112–113.
7. Ann and Barry Ulanov, *Religion and the Unconscious* (Philadelphia: Westminster Press, 1975), pp. 61–62.
8. C. G. Jung, *Psychology and Religion* (New Haven: Yale University Press, 1968), pp. 45–46.
9. *Ibid.*, p. 47.
10. *Ibid.*, p. 49.
11. *Ibid.*, p. 55.
12. Louis Dupré, "Mystical Experience of the Self," *Understanding Mysticism,* edited by Richard Woods, O.P. (New York: Doubleday, Image Books, 1980), p. 451.
13. Ann and Barry Ulanov, *Religion and the Unconscious* (Philadelphia: Westminster Press, 1975), p. 87.
14. *Ibid.*, p. 88.
15. Kenneth Wapnick, "Mysticism and Schizophrenia," *Understanding Mysticism,* edited by Richard Woods, O.P., p. 336.
16. *Ibid.*, p. 337.
17. *Ibid.*, p. 336.

18. Rom 8:26–27.

19. Carl G. Jung, *Modern Man in Search of a Soul,* translated by W. S. Dell and Cary F. Baynes (New York: Harvest Book, Harcourt, Brace and World, 1933), pp. 70–71.

20. Louis Dupré, "Mystical Experience of the Self," p. 451.

21. Meister Eckhart, Sermon. "Qui Audit Me, Non Condundetur," in *Meister Eckhart,* translated by Raymond Bernard Blakney (New York: Harper Brothers, 1957), p. 205.

22. Louis Dupré, p. 462, quoting Ruusbroec, *The Adornment of Spiritual Marriage,* translated by Wynsbench (New York: E. P. Dutton, 1916), p. 127.

23. William James, *Varieties of Religious Experience* (New York: Collier, Macmillan, 1961), p. 300.

24. James Fowler, "Toward a Developmental Perspective on Faith," *Religious Education,* Vol. LXIX, No. 2, March-April 1974, p. 207.

25. Karl Rahner, *Encyclopedia of Theology,* edited by Karl Rahner (London: Burns and Oates, 1975), p. 1010 as quoted by Wm. Johnston, *Inner Eye of Love* (San Francisco: Harper and Row, 1978), p. 31.

26. Wm. F. Lynch, S.J., *Images of Faith (An Explanation of Ironic Imagination)* (Notre Dame: University of Notre Dame, 1973), p. 8.

27. *Ibid.,* pp. 9–10.

28. C. G. Jung, *Psychology and Religion* (New Haven: Yale University Press, 1968), p. 75.

29. *Ibid.,* p. 80.

30. *Ibid.,* p. 113.

31. *Ibid.,* p. 114.

32. F. C. Happold, *The Journey Inward* (Atlanta: John Knox Press, 1968), p. 42.

33. Donald P. Gray, "Prayer: Passing Over and Coming Back," *Worship,* Vol. 48, No. 5, May 1974, pp. 300–301.

34. William Johnston, *The Inner Eye of Love* (San Francisco: Harper and Row, 1978), p. 100.

35. *Ibid.,* p. 101.

36. Donald L. Gelpi, S.J., *Experiencing God* (New York: Paulist Press, 1978), p. 334.

CHAPTER 4

The Shadow in the Personality Theory of Carl Jung

I once saw a two year old go off happily for a walk with his young father. A short time later both father and son returned in a state of near hysteria. The child was screaming uncontrollably, and the father was beside himself, not knowing how to calm his son. The child, he said, had discovered his shadow, had tried to run away from it, had tried to shake it off, had tried in desperation to lose, to stamp out this terrifying dark projection of himself. Failing, he was frightened as nothing had ever frightened him before.

It is a great parable, this little incident. In it one can see so much about that way of looking at the human person or aspect of the human person that Jungian psychology calls the shadow. "The term shadow refers to the part of the personality which has been repressed for the sake of the ego ideal. Since everything unconscious is projected, we encounter the shadow in projection—in our view of 'the other fellow.' "[1]

Here the child had been living totally unaware of this alter ego, this shadow that was so much his own. He had never noticed it before; he was unconscious of it. It had grown along with him, duplicating every inch of his expansion, every subtlety of his changing shape. It had been projected, more or less sharply, all around him in differing lengths and shades. Now, after all this time, he discovers it and is thrown into panic because he is irreversibly attached to it and it to him. No one can show him how to transform his shadow into rabbit's ears or a friendly "light show" yet because he is so shocked and fatalistic about this flat, vital, dark thing so close to him. There was nothing that his father could do to ease the pain or save him from this inevitable confrontation, so he brought him home for the support of his mother and the assembled kin.

I. Shadow as Typology

For all the years that each of us grows to adulthood, we make constant conscious and unconscious choices, creating our conscious personality, our particular ego. We are nudged and pushed along by the adults around us in our world, but there are inbuilt tendencies and attractions, some that we integrate into our personality, some that we reject. One of the most basic of all of these is that all of us have the potential for an outer life and an inner life, yet we seem to have an attraction for one over the other. Attracted to the outer life, some of us rush right into the outer world grabbing at everything, smiling at everyone, fearlessly flirting with, cajoling every object and person we encounter. We are drawn out to one thing after another. We welcome more and more colors, shapes, sounds; taste and chew, punch, squeeze, push and crush whatever falls into our path. We run into life, we make our "out there" choices or they almost seem to make us. We get up, get out, learn to walk, read and write, fight, play and work hard in our environments. We love to try new things and challenge new competitors, be they people or things.

All the while, we are unconsciously creating an undifferentiated other side. If we go for this outer world rather than an inner world, we leave the inner world in a somewhat untapped, shadowy condition. We create an introverted shadow side. There is an inner world that we abandon and repress in order to be so abandoned to extraversion.

Yet, there are others of us who don't have quite the same attraction for this outer world. Some of the human babies born on this earth have a sort of built-in *hesitation* about crawling or running out into all the objects and things and people in this outer world. They like to be, rather than do. They pause for reflection before plunging into activity. They will be more often alone or focus on one clothespin, or float on a raft or build a sandcastle, while others play games around them. They like to imagine, think, figure things out, contemplate. They need peace and privacy. They are as fascinated by the inner world of their own speculations, emotions, dreams, images and calculations as the earlier-described more extraverted people among us are drawn to the matter and space of the outer world. Theirs is a depth rather than breadth of perception and preoccupation, a depth rather than a breadth of personal relationships. These more introverted people can't seem to help, or be responsible for their preference any more than the extraverts are for theirs. It is a matter of gift, a matter of native tendency. The *real* world for them is within as the *real* world for the extravert is without. They get their energy from going within as the extravert gets energy from more and more external contacts.

> The extravert needs plenty of action, people, variety, conversation and opportunity to make a satisfying amount of noise. She is part of all she has met, and her grasp of the world depends on how much of it she has met. The introvert can use the same things—but not in such quantity. Too much togetherness leaves her drained. She needs a place where she can be alone and quietly concentrate on what interests her. For her sense of security she needs to be told about the underlying principles that hold the world together. . . . She will be much more at home in the world if it seems to be held together than if it seems to lie around in unrelated pieces.[2]

Relating the pieces in some inner dynamic "tapestries" or "solar system" seems to be the way of the introvert. But the introvert pays for that hesitancy toward the outer world by somewhat submerging her more extraverted side and her attitude of attraction to the variety and color and sheer multiplicity of the outer world. The introvert has a shadow extravert living inside as the extravert has a shadow introvert living inside. One attitude, either introversion or extraversion which is a true human potential for everyone has been somewhat sacrificed for the necessary development of a real gift or strength. In order for the extravert to grow into the more consciously extraverted person she was born to be, for which she has the natural capacity, concentration on the inner world has had to be quelled or minimized. In order for the introvert to become so at ease and adept at navigating in the inner realm where everything has its network and interpretation and shade of meaning, volume of interaction, expansion of experiences, and varieties of personalities have been neglected. One does not shake off or stamp out or lose this less developed side of oneself. It is there; it is part of one's unconscious personality, repressed, primitive, somewhat infantile, flat and devalued. One does all this unconsciously. It is an automatic mechanism. Automatic too is the projection of this shadow on others. We probably do not really like this weak side of ourselves though we are not even aware of its existence in us. What this translates into is that we don't like our shadow side when we see it well developed in the personality of others. To the more extraverted person the introvert looks "morose," "too serious," "egocentric." If the extravert were to catch himself giving too much attention to his more introverted side, he might worry why he was becoming so "morose," and just so the introvert begins to worry about "superficiality" in himself. This is one of the prices one pays for strong ego development. It is a one-sidedness with a sharply defined dark side.

In Jung's type theory which is his psychology of consciousness that we have been describing, there is more to one's conscious personality, of course, than these two attitudes of extraversion and introversion. There are functions which one develops at the expense of other functions. Again, a well-developed function which is such an asset in ego development means a corresponding unconscious, or shadow function. Like the frightened little boy's shadow, each of our shadows duplicate our every personality expansion, the subtleties of our changing shape.

In each of us two functions are easy for us to use and usually two are more difficult to operate out of. The ones that are not our gift tend to remain undeveloped, primitive, uncivilized, infantile. They are unconscious in us—part of our personal unconscious, part of our unconscious personality, part again of our shadow.

There are two functions of perception: sensing (using our senses) and intuition. If one relies primarily on the senses to gather information, intuition will tend to be unused, unnoticed and distrusted and therefore become part of one's shadow or inferior side. For the highly developed intuitive person who perceives through the unconscious, the senses will be underutilized and the facts that they offer will be seen as irrelevant. The intuitive person has and values her constant flashes of inspiration and insight. Sensing becomes part of her shadow.

The judgment functions are thinking and feeling. One develops thinking at the expense of feeling and feeling at the expense of thinking. One becomes as it were shadow of the other. If one has a gift for analytical, impersonal judgments and a strong logical reasoning power, if one is mostly guided by a firm unswerving commitment to principles, one's feeling function which values above all else harmonious human contacts or personal values will tend to be pushed under for the sake of one's preferred thinking function. The opposite will happen with a highly developed feeler.

The pairs are: sensing and intuition, functions of perception; thinking and feeling, functions of judgment. Jung's type theory is that each of us with a healthy ego development will most likely have one function of these four most highly developed and one from the other pair as a helping function. The opposite of the most highly developed or primary function will be least developed or the inferior function. Our introversion or extraversion will be colored by these preferred functions. Therefore, an Extraverted Thinking type will have a shadow that looks like an undeveloped, uncvilized introverted feeling type. When this person makes a judgment, not based on her highly developed conscious side but through introverted feeling, it will be a childish, primitive kind of judgment.

> A person's type is the product of conscious orientation to life: habitual purposeful ways of using one's mind—habitual because they seem good and trustworthy. The shadow is something that happens when a person isn't looking.[3]

In the extraverted thinking type, introverted feeling will not look as it does in the person whose ego or conscious personality is characterized by introverted feeling. It will, when it is not integrated, express itself in an inferior way. Such an expression may be an overwhelming fear of being alone and a terrible fear of being rejected. It can grasp one emotionally, and so, for example, one ordinarily impersonal, logical, thinking type in the grips of her shadow showed her extreme hurt at having been left out of a party of intimate friends in which she had no reason for being included except perhaps some physical proximity. This same person on another occasion when she was part of the group to which she was invited asked to include two people who were strangers to the group and turned the dinner into a business meeting—another example of her inferior feeling, her shadow. Besides such undifferentiated kinds of feeling decisions, this shadow may be expressed in depressions, periods when the thinker is overwhelmed with gloom.

The introverted feeling type will, on the other hand, have a shadow of extraverted thinking. He will always find himself overwhelmed by too many ideas, too many facts, too much material. The result will be oversimplification or "missing logical links." In speaking, I have seen such a person start expressing his thoughts on a subject and apparently get lost before making a logical conclusion to his thought. Because of their strong attachment to inner ideals, introverted feeling types may be domineering and dogmatic in expressing opinions which run far beyond their real certitude. This type may misinterpret another's preoccupation and silence as a personal snub and so manufacture a whole inner drama, deciding that he has offended the other in some way. Since peace and harmony in relationships is such a priority, the feeler may then become defensive and obsessed with ways of reinstating himself in the other's good graces. He has projected his inferior thinking on the other whose absorption had nothing at all to do with him.

In general, the shadow of sensing types will express itself in foreboding, expectations of catastrophe; weird visions of apocalyptic disaster may haunt them because their intuition is so poorly adapted. Intuitives, on the other hand, will have their problems with the material world. Perhaps some form of greed, acquisitiveness or pleasure-seeking will characterize them. Their shadow will manifest itself in an inferior grasp of space and time and facts in general. They cannot see the trees for the forest. Their bodies may be neglected as a result of inferior sensing.

All these are very vague general kinds of pointers to the kinds of possible manifestations of the shadow that can grip any one of us because of our typology. When we notice that our shadow acts, we tend to say, "I wasn't myself. I don't know what got into me!" But most of the time our shadow acts without our even noticing. We are, as it were gripped, possessed. This shadow, this aspect of our personal unconscious is a real and powerful part of our personality, however much we deny it as part of us. "Closer examination of the inferiorities constituting the shadow reveal that they have an emotional nature, a kind of autonomy and accordingly an obsessive or better, possessive quality."[4]

Repression gives one the image of a pressure from above that will not hold forever. The repressed contents will move out sometime. We have been discussing some of the contents of the personal unconscious referred to by Jung as the shadow and some hints as to ways the shadow is operative, if unconsciously, in the personality. Before discussing ways in which one's shadow can be recognized and named further so that it can be transformed and integrated into the conscious personality, before exploring ways in which it can be included into a higher consciousness once ego development is secure in the mature adult, it is important to realize that there is much more to the shadow than the undeveloped attitude and the inferior functions.

II. Shadow as Taboo

In each of our childhood homes there were feelings, behaviors and stances that were approved and those that were taboo. We had assimilated an acceptable set of these before we ever knew there could be another way to be. Ours was a kissing or not kissing family. There was noise or quiet, hospitality or aloofness, an ethnic body language, effusive or restrained. There was roughness or gentility, order or chaos or something in between; cleanliness or casualness, prodigality or frugality, abundance of food or famine, an ethnic taste and degree of care in preparation. There was expression of anger or repression of anger, respect or irreverence, beauty or ugliness, some type of music or lack of it, warmth or coldness, careful etiquette or little of it, confidence or shyness, violence or non-violence, competition or accommodation. One could go on indefinitely listing such opposites in expectations, one of which became part of one's conscious personality and then imagine its opposite as part of one's shadow, one's unconscious, the unlived personality in each of us, a real potential in each of us. When we have an emotional reaction to someone whose "way" contradicts our own, to what degree are we projecting our own distaste for that repressed, undeveloped "way" that is our own shadow within?

In dwelling first on the more neutral aspects of what Jung called the shadow, I have attempted to differentiate the shadow from an immediate connection with moral evil. Such identification of the shadow and moral evil is too simplistic, though in some ways it can now be seen that just like our frightened little boy, we can see these really neutral human parts of ourselves as "evil" and can work up a real hatred for them in ourselves and others. People have killed and been killed in this kind of shadow conflict over typology or taste.

When Jung talks about the integration of the shadow into the conscious personality as the beginning of the way to wholeness in the second half of life, the assimilation of these more neutral or truly good human potentialities will be more easily understood and accepted as a moral responsibility than the equally moral responsibility of the recognition and befriending of what are the truly objective evil aspects of our own shadow. The Shadow of the truly morally evil person, the criminal, will, of course, also be all potentially *good* qualities that such a person surpressed in developing a consciously evil personality.

> What is the shadow then?
>
> The psychological definition of the shadow which we must bear in mind before going into our material can vary greatly and is not as simple as we generally assume. In Jungian psychology, we generally define the shadow as the personification of certain aspects of the unconscious personality, which could be added to the ego complex but, for various reasons, are not. We might, therefore, say that the shadow is the dark unlived and repressed side of the ego complex, but this is only partly true. Dr. Jung, who hates it when his pupils are too literal minded and cling to his concepts and make a system out of them and quote him without knowing exactly what they are saying, once in a discussion threw all this over and said, "This is all nonsense! The shadow is simply the whole unconscious."[5]

In saying this, Jung was not only pointing out the mystery and vastness of the shadow but he was pointing us back to the individual. He was pointing each of us back to our own individual development, to look for "my" shadow rather than "the" shadow. To the extent that I have to be right and therefore good, the others, "*they*" or "*he*" or "*she*," are the ones who are wrong and so evil. To this extent, I have not met my shadow. But this came about as I developed through the interaction of my unique potentials with my individual environments. I found myself to be "right" if I fit in and "wrong" whenever I didn't. What didn't "fit in" in me became unconscious.

> Those elements of the individuality which are too much at variance with accepted personal values cannot seemingly be incorporated into the image which the ego has of itself. They therefore become subject to repression. They do not disappear, however; they continue to function as an unseen alter ego which seems to be outside oneself—in other words, as the shadow. Ego development rests upon repressing the "wrong" or "evil" and furthering the "good." The ego cannot become strong unless we first learn collective taboos, accept superego values and personal values and identify with collective moral standards.[6]

Human beings are not morally indifferent, nor amoral. There seems to be built in tendency to "shoulds" to create collective moral standards and to introduce each new member of the race to these collective standards. In our Western culture, the Judaeo-Christian ethic has evolved in some detail in its evaluation of motivations and behaviors and has etched some very intricate "do's" and dont's. If we grew up learning this morality, perhaps passing through various stages on our moral reasoning and with a certain amount of parallel growth in our moral behavior, we see ourselves as truly moral persons. We identify with the "good guys and girls" in the dramas we see, and we jeer at the villains. In our daily life, we shake our heads and are shocked at the criminals whose actions fill our newspapers or TV screens. We vote for stricter penalties for crimes and for prison reform and want to be known as the honest, upright citizens that we are.

Beyond this, we may even work against injustice in the world and make personal sacrifices to help establish a more just society. We may be concerned with ecology and starvation and nuclear disarmament and do whatever we can in behalf of such causes.

In our personal lives, we may try to practice great charity and forgiveness and really try to grow in virtue. We may have learned the commandments and try to live them in minute detail. We may be very aware of the capital sins and be working to eliminate any traces of them from our lives. In place of pride we may try to practice humility; in place of avarice, we may strive to be generous. Rather than gluttony, we may strive to be a model of sobriety and asceticism. We may try to eliminate lust and live in great chastity. We may try to eliminate the least trace of envy and grow in magnanimity. We may never allow an angry moment but strive always to be meek. Sloth may seem banished completely by diligence and hard work.

When we fail, even slightly, we may be contrite and very shocked because we are really virtuous persons. All of this is an attempt to spell out, however sketchily, the kind of moral standards that define the kind of ego ideal we have set before us and set for ourselves. And though we may talk about moral decay and see plenty of it in the media and in real life all around us, we still do not admire it as we do the real "striving to be good" heroines and heroes who populate most of our media and most of our neighborhoods.

One result of our emphasis on our own moral perfection is that we honestly believe that we are *only* this ego self and give no thought to the reality of our weak side. The theory that the shadow of each of these virtues is there in our own unconscious personality is something that we find a surprising thought. The discovery of the unconscious here again shows itself to be one of the most important and far-reaching discoveries of modern times. Not suspecting this unconscious side, it is as though we had eliminated all this ugliness and evil and only had this virtuous self. Yet deep down we know that our experience is really different.

> We think we have successfully got rid of these inferior, undesirable tendencies when in fact all that happened is that they have been pushed into the background and stored away in the dark closets of our being, all the while continuing very much alive. Our conformity to what is expected of us leads us to behave in the acceptable way and much that is rightly a part of the human personality gets pushed away into unconsciousness. This mechanism of forgetting or repressing works so well and is often so successful that many people come to believe that they *are* exactly as they appear to be, and that frequently proves to be disastrous.[7]

There is still within us the potential for each of the sins that we have so carefully tried to eliminate. Experience shows us this is true. When we are really honest with ourselves we know that pride, avarice, gluttony, lust, envy, anger and sloth can rise up and grip us. If we are honest we know that the commandments point to potentials that we still have. The "shalt nots" are there because the opposite is a real possibility for me. Any of us really could steal another's husband or wife or take a life.

The idea that temptations come from the "world," the "flesh" and the "devil" seemed to put the source of our weakness somewhere outside. Even the flesh in our recent more dualistic way of seeing was "outside" ourselves. Late Christianity has refined morality to a beautiful ideal and "trained" the will to a fine-tuned instrument. Yet there is, as a result of such strong identification with these beautiful ideals, a repressed, dark side which the more blinded our virtue makes us to it, the longer will be the shadow it casts.

> If an individual is unaware of his shadow being completely identified with his conscious personality, he will be entirely convinced of his own rectitude. The elements of his own nature which cannot be accommodated to his shining personality will be projected on someone in his immediate environment, a brother, son, friend, or, more often a bête noire, the associate whom he particularly dislikes whose faults he cannot avoid seeing and criticizing on every occasion, in season and out. And here we often see a very strange effect of unconsciousness. For the one on whom the shadow has fallen is unavoidably influenced in an unconscious way by the projection, and if the two people are closely connected the recipient of the projection may be constrained to live the negative role projected upon him.[8]

All the vices that we have repressed will be seen outside in other people, and this *is* a terrible vice. We see ourselves as "good" and others as the "evil" ones. We seem to be incapable of such evil because we are projecting it on "them." We are suspicious of each of "them." Even when others do objective evil, our shadow adds to their genuine evil its own darkness so as to make us shine more brightly. In this way we come out "smelling like roses." Every real evil done by another serves to distance us further, move us up above the common herd. To the degree that this is so, the love of neighbor that we have is more condescension than compassion born of common humanity. Such condescension can never be true love. The paradox of our emphasis on Christian perfection is that the human love at the heart of Christianity is warped by our failure to admit to our own unconscious weak and even evil side. The paradox is, further, that the evil side, repressed within, is less than its projection makes it and that withdrawing projections and admitting one's own evil weakens the evil, even transforms it and gives new energy for love of self and others. If one cannot try to love what became weak, childish, undeveloped, ugly in oneself for the sake of all one's strengths, if one cannot love the side of oneself that paid for one's developed ego by its neglect and diminishment, how can one love oneself? And if one cannot really love oneself, how can one love the God who somehow made humanity this way? How can one love and identify with the God who in Jesus spent most of his energy and called his disciples to the weak things of the world? How can one love one's neighbor as oneself?

It has taken centuries to spell out the details of the *conscious* love of self, God and neighbor. We are only at the beginning of trying to spell out what it means to love the unconscioius, especially as it is manifest in one's shadow. We know that love means many things in dealing with another. It can be tender or tough. We must come to know our own shadow and follow our inner wisdom as to the shapes its love will take.

III. Knowing One's Shadow

Coming to know the shadow is really the spirituality of the second half of life. The first half of one's life, if one develops in a healthy and moral way, is given over to ego building, and while that is going on shadows are necessarily being repressed and ignored. As in the first half of life we watched for our external faults and examined our conscience for moral shortcomings in order to grow in adaptation, in will power, and in virtue, our adventure now will be to pay attention to the much more subtle manifestations of the shadow. A path can be broadly outlined by inferring from what we know of our conscious personality where to look for our inferior sides. The integration of the opposite typological attitude and functions can be a great adventure in the second half of life.

When at mid-life one reaches the "top of the ladder" to find, as people in mid-life often feel, that the ladder is against the wrong roof, one can still turn around and see what personality has been developed by climbing that ladder. What is the ego like that was built up in the first half of life? What are the opposite chararceristics of such an ego? What are the opposite characteristics of one's one-sidedness? What is the unlived side that can now emerge? How can I become more my true self, the self that is God's image and includes so much more than this conscious ego? How can I become more my true self by integrating morc introversion or extraversion? How can I become more my true self by integrating my undeveloped, inferior functions? How can I become more my true self by rediscovering such parts of myself as sincerity, gaiety, casualness or firmness that got repressed somewhere in youth for the sake of other qualities that were then seen as more needed in my personality? How can I become more my true self by unleashing other qualities that were never allowed to have their play in my personality? How can I realize the energies of the vices I have suppressed? How, most importantly, can I do these things and not be inundated by the unconscious and lose my hard-built ego?

But, first, how can I discover these potentials that are real and life-giving for me? How can I find my own shadow? In Jung's theory, one important place to look is in one's dreams. The shadow manifests itself in one's dreams as a person of one's own sex. This primitive part of oneself is personified by a despised or inferior person, by someone who in some way is adverse or threatening to one, or in some way an enemy. One can look to one's dreams to give direction as to one's truly unconscious shadow self. Edward Whitmont tells the story of a man who is confronted in a dream with a part of his personality that he is unaware of. This dreamer is very liberal, tolerant and broad-minded, or at least he assumes that he is. He dreams: "Coming home, I find that my apartment is occupied by a fascist who, with his militia, has turned everything upside down. He has arrested everybody in the house and put them in chains. The place is in shambles."[9] Here the progressive broad-minded dreamer is notified that there is a fascist, a totalitarian dictator in his house, that is, in his personality makeup. This quality which demands blind compliance has chained most of his lively faculties and created havoc. Our dreamer is, of course a fascist hater and will always grow very emotional and excited when the word is mentioned in his presence.

Whitmont tells another story about a daughter-in-law who sees in her mother-in-law qualities which are having a negative effect on her marriage. In a dream, she sees a spotlight on herself, not on her mother-in-law, and realizes that it was the identical qualities in her that were preventing her from reaching her husband. "Since she cannot see herself as she truly is she also cannot see her mother-in-law as a human being and therefore cannot deal adequately with the obstructionist tactics which she indeed does use."[10]

One can perhaps encounter one's shadow by drawing up a list of qualities one particularly dislikes in others. Or one can think of a person one finds particular difficulty in getting along with, someone whom one finds despicable and unbearable. Then one can try to see where these qualities might be present in oneself. "A projection invariably blurs our own view of the other person. Even when the projected qualities happen to be real qualities of the other person . . . the affect reaction which marks the projection points to the affect toned complex in *us* which blurs our vision and interferes with our capacity to see objectively and relate humanly."[11]

Emotional reactions to other individuals or to a certain group should make us suspect of an unconscious involvement; for example an extremely virtuous woman is very concerned with "fallen girls" or someone has an extreme contempt for drunkards or for politicians. Emotion, says Jung, is "not an activity of the individual but something that happens to him. Affects occur usually where adaptation is weakest and at the same time they reveal the reason for its weakness, namely a certain degree of inferiority and the existence of a lower level of personality."[12]

Another way of observing the working of the shadow is when one produces an effect which one did not intend. Someone may react to a simple statement one has made with the complaint, "It isn't what you said; it's the way you said it that hurt." Here one intended to say something that was perhaps sympathetic or pleasant and phrased it, or said it, with an intonation that produced the opposite effect. It is also the shadow rather than the ego who acts, when one blunders over some task one would expect to perform easily and correctly. Something similar may be going on when one performs an impulsive or inadvertent but non-characteristic action. It may even be seen when one is not living up to one's potential and so is projecting unlived good qualities onto someone else who "can do no wrong" and about whose perfection one has an unreal and inflated opinion.

Sometimes in discovering our shadow, we will be discovering a shortcoming that we should overcome—but sometimes the shadow will reveal a meaningful bit of life that we should accept and begin to live. Marie-Louise Von Franz gives an example of a very introverted, disciplined man who dreamed of a loudly laughing friend from childhood and three beautiful, strong horses escaping from military service. In his case, it seemed that both were shadow figures revealing parts of himself that now needed to be integrated. The childhood friend "probably stands for the dreamer's neglected capacity for enjoying life and for his extraverted shadow side. . . . The horses may have escaped from military service, that is, from the conscious discipline that had hitherto characterized his life."[13] Sometimes the shadow is calling to the ego to give up some of its pride and priggishness and begin to integrate and live something that seems to be dark but actually may not be. Thus, getting in touch with one's shadow can present one with no small number of ethical problems, and yet not getting in touch with one's shadow, especially in the second half of life, is a great failure in moral responsibility and can have dire consequences not only for oneself and one's immediate neighbors but for the whole of society.

Collective shadow is obviously even more destructive than personal shadow. The projection of the German shadow on the Jews under Nazism, the shadow of the white race on the blacks, and the shadow of the settlers of the new world on the native Americans are classic examples. The power of a collective shadow of a group on an individual, who when left alone would never do what she will be drawn into doing as part of the mass caught in mob mentality, is another example of the power of the collective shadow.

In growing up and developing our conscious ego we are each, of course, influenced by the collective shadows in the society of which we are a part. Ageism, sexism, racism, the work ethic, and materialism may all have been part of our Western culture that any of us imbibed along with untold other dark qualities.

It is obvious that the shadow can never be wholly eliminated nor wholly integrated. We will always have a dark side. The important attitude toward the shadow is to acknowledge its presence, to learn from it and never to disown or ignore it.

> The adequate question therefore never is: Have I a shadow problem? Have I a negative side? But rather: Where does it happen to be right now? When we cannot see it, it is time to beware! And it is helpful to remember Jung's formulation that a complex is not pathological per se. It becomes pathological only when we assume that we do not have it; because then it has us.[14]

Notes

1. Edward C. Whitmont, *The Symbolic Quest* (New Jersey: Princeton University Press, 1969) p. 160.

2. Isabel Briggs Myers with Peter B. Myers, *Gifts Differing* (Palo Alto, California: Consulting Psychologists Press, Inc., 1980), p. 177.

3. *Ibid.*, p. 85.

4. C.G. Jung, *Aion*, translated by R.F.C. Hull (New Jersey: Princeton University Press, Bollingen Series XX, 1959), p. 8.

5. Marie Louise Von Franz, *Shadow and Evil in Fairytales* (Zurich: Spring Publications, 1974), p. 5.

6. Edward C. Whitmont, *The Symbolic Quest*, p. 163.

7. William A. Miller, *Why Do Christians Break Down?* (Minneapolis: Augsburg Publishing House, 1973), p. 59.

8. M. Esther Harding, *The I and the Not I* (New Jersey: Princeton University Press, Bollingen Series XXIX, 1965), p. 78.

9. Edward C. Whitmont, *The Symbolic Quest*, pp. 161–162.

10. *Ibid.*, p. 161.

11. *Ibid.*

12. C.G. Jung, *Aion*, pp. 8–9.

13. Marie Louise Von Franz, "The Process of Individuation," *Man and His Symbols*, edited by C.G. Jung (New York: Doubleday, 1964), p. 170.

14. Edward C. Whitmont, *The Symbolic Quest*, p. 168.

CHAPTER 5

The Shadow and Prayer in the Second Half of Life

I. Letting Go into the Other

Prayer is a whole person activity. It is a mysterious letting go "into" or "with" the Other. It is a transcendency of oneself and at the same time a gathering together of oneself, a being with one's Self. I am rushing around, caring for my life, accomplishing my things, being responsible, getting things done, worrying about not getting things done. I am pressured, hassled, distracted, in pain, grieving, or I am concentrating, satisfied with an achievement, rejoicing at an unexpected boon when, in an instant, I switch, as it were, out of myself or is it "into" myself and for a few or many seconds or minutes let go in God in prayer. I become aware of a more than me, a beyond all this. I transcend everything but move all of it into transcendence. Here and now opens out to timelessness and beyond space when I pray. As I move in this other realm however, I am not in a foreign, threatening place. I am at home. What must be an abyss beyond clocks and calendars and the horizons of my well trodden little world is not a vacuum or ultimately fearful but comfortable, even as it is challenging and awesome and sometimes a place of struggle. I am somewhere where myself is known. I am in an unknown region that somehow I know.

I am "E.T." and my being is answered and energized by moving out, calling out, "phoning home". I know that I am someone sought and valued. Home is accessible, so accessible that my "real" life in time and space can often feel more foreign.

Praying is coming out into the open, coming before God as I am. There can be no pretense in real prayer. The bright light of the Love who creates me touches every conscious and shadowy place in me. I must come to pray naked and relax in being only who I am and infinitely loved. God loves *me* unconditionally.

Our God who is incarnate in Jesus has been becoming incarnated in creation from the beginning, and dwells among us still, the Spirit of Christ, vivifying all human flesh and earthly human enterprise. No created being is base to God. Each of us lives and moves and has being in mutuality with this God. Our unity and our differentiation flows from this same source. Thus, it is only possible to pray, to be with God in our own flesh. We have, each of us, grown out of and contain the clay and the chaos. Our reality is awesome animal quickened by incredible psyche and spirit. It is impossible to really pray, to be with God who is our origin and end and deny the smallest part of our real selves. We cannot come to God as pure spirit. We can only be real, and at this point in history we know that reality, that Self, to include our evolutionary roots, our conscious and unconscious, our ego and our shadow.

Too often we try to pray like a mother playing peek-a-boo with her baby. We cover our faces with our hands and say, "All gone." We deny and suppress whole areas of ourselves so that we "can pray." However, like the hermits who went to the desert to escape evil and be with God, we are confronted with visions of seductive dancing girls or lurid tempters. When any tempters, lurid or other, come with us into the silence of prayer, we are well advised to suspect our own shadow and to ask what the Spirit of God wants to speak in me now. In this age when we are cut off from our earthly roots, so suspect of what is not rational and measurable, so blind to symbol, so fearful of emotion, it may well be that such "distractions" in prayer are the groans of the Spirit within, shackled in our unlived life.

> If we can let ourselves go in prayer and speak all that is in our minds and hearts, if we can sit quietly and bear the silence, we will hear all the bits and pieces of ourselves crowding in on us, pleading for our attention. Prayer's confession begins with this racket, for prayer is noisy with all the parts of us demanding to be heard. The clamor is the sound of the great river of being flowing in us. This is what depth psychologists call "primary process thinking," that level of our psyche's functioning that leads straight to the working of our souls.[1]

There are so many shadows we try to hide from God and so abort both worship and the fruit of prayer. For example, fear and aggression are inbuilt human survival mechanisms, defenses against suffering and death. God knows them. They are part of the way we are made. Desire and sex are for growth of the Self and the race. God knows them. They are part of how we are made. Like everything else that is, all these are potentials for good and evil. They are all deeply connected therefore to our typology and taboos. If prayer is a whole person activity, if we are at home here in prayer, then even our most violent and obscene fantasies need to be laid open before God, not just shoved away into some black hole of denial or suppression, so that we can then "pray."

If there is a volcano within me overflowing in fantasies of hot hate, I do well to do what the psalmist did: lay bare my hate before God. Screaming my hate before God is the exact opposite of choosing my hate as my god and collapsing into it, living out of it and living it out. I think that I cannot pray my shadow side, that I would profane my prayer or blaspheme. Yet, unless I do pray my shadow side as it exists and as it surfaces, *I* am not praying, I am not with the true God. I am lying to a lie. I am boasting before an idol of my own making. I am the Pharisee who boasted of his justice and so could not be heard and went away unjustified.

> He then spoke this parable addressed to those who believed in their own self-righteousness while holding everyone else in contempt: "Two men went up to the temple to pray; one a Pharisee, the other a tax collector. The Pharisee with head unbowed prayed in this fashion: "I give you thanks, O God, that I am not like the rest of men—grasping, crooked, adulterous—or even like this tax-collector. I fast twice a week. I pay tithes on all I possess." The other man, however, kept his distance, not even daring to raise his eyes to heaven. All he did was beat his breast and say, "O God, be merciful to me, a sinner." Believe me, this man went home from the temple justified but the other did not. For everyone who exalts himself shall be humbled while he who humbles himself shall be exalted" (Lk 17:9–14).

Jung's theory of the shadow can tell us much about being exalted by humbling oneself and about contacting God and worshiping God by acknowledging more and more elements of our true Self. On the other hand, praying opens the Shadow, the very personal and collective out to the more of God. God's mercy is the abyss which contains all, holds all, transforms all.

Jung seems to describe from a psychological perspective something of what is going on when one prays. Without reducing prayer to an encounter with the unconscious, there is at least an analogy between his description of moving beyond the conscious and this letting go into God of prayer. In Jung's theory, the unconscious is both familiar and foreign territory. It is one's shadow personality, and so it is one's unlived potential, the other side of one's conscious personality; yet it is collective, and so it is much more. As previously discussed, Jung's broadest meaning for the shadow is the "whole unconscious." This is understandable since Jung saw the shadow as potential good within the individual as well as potential evil, and potential good within the collective as well as potential evil. My shadow is very much me. The shadow of the race is very much mine also. The darkness of the shadow can be the source of greatest light, the strangeness of the shadow can become an intimate experience of what is closest to me, and so, on recognition, most familiar. What appears to be threatening or taboo can be appropriated as true growth toward individuation. What appears to be adverse can be part of my undiscovered Self. This unconscious realm is always there for one to be with. However, when one has acquired the ego strength of the first half of life, the encounter is even more enriching. Communication with this shadow and integration of it into one's conscious personality is the real work of the second half of life.

Each night as one dreams, one enters this shadow world, one lets go the day of one's conscious life and experiences oneself in a whole new way. There is both the familiar and the unfamiliar in one's dreams. I recognize myself and my feelings. It is my frustrations, my aggressions, my dreads, my soarings, my potentials that I encounter. There are often people from my world, and some things about the places are familiar, and yet, the confusions of sequence and lack of continuity and congruity, the beyond time and space and logic make this at the same time a foreign world. This (almost) third of one's life when one sleeps and dreams is part of one's experience of living. The necessity of sleep for physical health and survival is taken for granted. The necessity of dreams for psychic growth is only now beginning to be taken seriously. The importance of dreams to spiritual growth is another area for exploration. It is only now that we are seeing that anthropology is putting us in contact with the connection between our dreams and our cultural myths, and the connection between our myths and our philosophies and theologies of life.

Myths are great poems. When they are thought of as just untruths or as primitive historical tales, they are being misread and aborted. Myths speak not of historical facts but of themes of the inner world of imagination, truths of our very being and our universe.

We know now that many dream symbols appear cross-culturally. Jung first recognized the archetypes of the collective unconscious in their manifestation in dreams, his own and those of his patients, and then in dreams and myths of all the different peoples he studied. Joseph Campbell's four volume work on world myths, *Masks of God*, is confirmation of Jung's theories.

> All my life, as a student of mythologies, I have been working with these archetypes and I can tell you they do exist and are the same all over the world. In the various traditions they are variously represented. . . . The myths and rites will be given different interpretations, different rational applications, different social customs to validate and enforce. And yet the archetypal, essential forms are the same—often stunningly so. And so what then *are* they? The psychologist who has best dealt with these, best described and best interpreted them is Carl G. Jung, who terms then "archetypes of the collective unconscious."[2]

According to Jung the contents of the archetypes change in every age but the forms or patterns appearing and reappearing are the same. These archetypes are the expression of an inherited human biology and psychology as instincts are in animals. "Like the nest of a bird, a mythology is fashioned of materials drawn from the local environment, apparently altogether consciously, but according to an architecture unconsciously dictated from within.[3]

So the grand characters and themes of our mythologies and, before them, of at least some of our dreams are eternal and transcultural. They speak directly to the perennial mysteries of our lives: human love and human suffering, birth, death and transitions, beginnings and endings and transformations. Our myths, then, are transpersonal and yet they are utterly personal, for each of us participates in this collective. Living myths have great power to vivify an individual and a culture. They are doorways to the wonder, both terrifying and fascinating, of ourselves and the whole universe. They are doorways from a faith perspective to the experience of the Holy because they can provide the common images which each individual uniquely embodies in his or her own story as a story of God. Such a truly personal appropriation is an act of self-transcendence rooted in one's own psyche and so can be a numinous kind of experience characterized by "the highest appreciation" (Jung's definition of a religious experience). Mandalas are symbols of wholeness. Paradise is a symbol of wholeness. The mandala, paridisal, resolution, vision dreams which Jung records as "meaning everything" to those who had them, effected these kinds of transformations, integrations, conversions, healings in the dreamer.

The Hebrew and Christian Scriptures use these same kinds of mandala or wholeness or completion symbols: paradise, ladder from earth to heaven, lion and lamb, transfiguration, heavenly Jerusalem, the new heaven and the new earth. The mysterious otherness and numinosity of such symbols met in dreams and so, strangely yet vaguely familiar when met in Scripture, fascinate and touch a chord within. We have all experienced the shadow world in sleep and so know this unconscious and its symbols and archetypes, which Jung speaks of, as part of our own experience.

But there is in waking too the possibility of contact with this unconscious. There is ongoing in the twilight zone of my psyche the stream of images which I can sometimes "catch by the tail" when I advert to them, and bring them to consciousness. This is called primary process or symbolic thinking. It goes before my thoughts and concepts and colors all of them, weighting each one with its special value from my history and prehistory. Computers are showing us secondary process or directed thought cut off from evaluation. Raw data unnuanced by human valuing is screened by the computer. Contrasted with this, primary process thinking is that which contains within itself

> a mixture of the products of the unconscious expressed in the language of dreams, myths and fantasies and in those forms of human communication which draw directly upon image and affect, such as poetry, painting, music, religion, myth, fable and even psychoanalytical ritual.[4]

Jung maintained and saw as important that non-directed or primary process thinking continues always to undergird the directed thinking of consciousness. In early childhood the ego, as the center of consciousness, develops out of the matrix of unconsciousness, just so, in the same way,

> non-directed thinking is the natural given life of the psyche from which is formed the directed thinking of consciousness. . . . Non-directed thinking is a natural phenomenon necessary to the functioning of the human psyche. It turns pathological only when it continues to dominate a person's mental functioning to the exclusion of directed thought, as in schizophrenia, for example.[5]

So we can experience this commerce between our conscious and unconscious selves not only when we dream but in all those moments when we "let go" of conscious processes and concerns. Relaxation response and meditation techniques of all kinds are teaching us the importance of such letting go for our physical and psychic health. Allowing oneself to go with one's inner images or following one's guided imagery rests the whole person and gives new life and energy. Conversely, attempting to eliminate images is another way to touch one's inner depths and can often produce the same deep renewal and energizing. Again, in this kind of contacting of the inner Self there is the same possibility of experiencing in one's own primary process thinking the same kinds of images and symbols that are the raw material for the symbols that populate the iconography of the world's religions.

II. Light and Darkness

As one enters this world within, however, one does not invariably move into a place of peace and tranquility. In sleep, one can have a dream that is a nightmare. "A nightmare is any dream from which we wake ourselves up in fear. The reason so few people have dreams in which they actually die may be that they usually wake themselves up before this can happen."[6] In dreams and in meditation too, we can and do encounter symbols that seem to be hostile, dangerous, destructive and evil forces. These forces take different shapes. Some are personalities from our own life history, people who are adverse to us. Some are bestial, primitive monsters of our own manufacture or composites of ugly creatures, universal symbols, like snakes or dragons or demons, which appear traditionally as enemies in the myths of all nations.

> We cannot escape meeting the dark forces in us, and soon, when we set out to encounter the figures of our inner world, not only is there a negative side of our personality residing in the shadow figure but the entire realm of the collective unconscious has potentially destructive power and requires a cautious approach. Anyone whose ego consciousness, for a period of time, has been overwhelmed by unconscious forces can vouch for the power within us.[7]

Potentially destructive or not, one cannot continue the individuation process in the second half of life without such an inward movement. It is the encounter with the shadow that is the gateway to the process of becoming one's own true Self in the second half of life. Integration of more and more of one's unconscious into one's conscious life means a new relationship, not only with one's personal shadow but also with all those forces represented by the collective shadows and universal symbolisms of evil.

Ego development has of necessity resulted in unconscious onesidedness. Onesidedness in its blindness is truly blind to the other side, to the possible riches and goodness of the other side. The extravert has become a more and more healthy and real extravert by denying again and again her introverted side. The Puritan becomes more and more Puritan by denying his pleasure-seeking play side; the Player by denying and repressing his Puritan becomes more the Player. The activist has despised the mystic within, and the mystic his own activism. Needless to say projection has occurred. Onesidedness unconsciously causes pain and does evil just because of being unconscious of, and blind to, the other side. It is very often the surfacing of just such evil, the experience of guilt for one's blind evil that begins this part of the individuation process.

> The ego is a sleepy bear who prefers to hibernate. Few people become conscious without having to become conscious, without being driven to it by necessity. And this is where evil comes in. For the most part, it is only when people encounter evil in some form—as pain, loss of mean-

> ing or something that appears to be threatening or destructive to them—that they begin to find their way to consciousness.[8]

Not only is this assimilation of personal shadow material necessary for growth toward individuation but the overall re-evaluation of all good and evil is very important to the whole second half of life. One does not reach mid-life without having been shocked into the awareness of the reality of evil, both within oneself and one's whole society and culture. Staring into the face of evil without losing one's human potential for living on and loving without cynicism, one needs the underpinning of a myth that can encompass evil, this negative shadow, and not be devoured by it. One needs a way to make such a myth operative and available to oneself again and again. The God myth in its Judaeo-Christian form is one that has had this kind of power for thousands of years and it still can grip us this way. These myths have had such great spiritual power and have effected such great spiritual growth because they express so completely the mystery within the heart of humanity and the elements of every human story.

Prayer is the dynamic relationship each of us has to the mystery present in those myths. Prayer can be again and again the operative appropriation and activation of the power in them. Prayer is one's active and passive involvement with the God of these great myths, with that God's kaleidoscopic manifestations in the myriad aspects of those myths. Prayer is whole-person attentiveness to God—God revealed, manifested or named by the rich word, "God," or the other names and manifestations: Creator, Love, Good, Truth, Beauty, One, Mystery, Savior, Spirit, Shepherd, Father, Mother, Emmanuel, Wisdom, Flame, Breath, Burning Bush, Rock, Key of David, Messiah, Lion of Judah, Son of Man, God Man, Christ, Kingdom, Alpha, Omega, Word Made Flesh, Resurrection, Life, Redeemer.

One can contact and appropriate the power of the myth, one can pray, by looking with faith on any revelation of God in the beauty around one. Such prayer can be the unverbalized leap of one's heart in wonder. One can pray by listening to the thunder and harshness of a storm or the whisper of a breeze. One can light a candle, pay attention to one's breathing, hold a rock, contemplate a mother or a father with a child, trim a vine, or read, think about or lose oneself in any fragment of the Bible's riches as a way of praying. Prayer is reaching for God by contacting any part of the images or symbols touching any part of this God myth: prodigal son, good Samaritan, pearl of great price, Eucharist, Mother of God, Virgin, Christmas, Easter, hymns, saints, crosses, stars of David. As light shining through any fragment of a holograph will reproduce the whole image, each element of this God myth contains the whole of it and has the power of the whole of it.

As though caught in the heart of a multi-faceted crystal palace, wherever evil looks, one of these aspects of the God story is there to reflect it back in a transformed image, a diminished image, because there is background and so containment. Prodigals and their "perfect" but loveless older brothers are run toward by their Father. A robber's victims are good Samaritaned, and Samaritan outcasts are praised. Red Seas mire pursuing chariot wheels, executioners' crosses turn gold and are honored. Virgins give birth, death gives way to resurrection, suffering redeems. The fact that there remain manifestations of the good, the true and the beautiful in the midst of the holocaust diminishes the success of the very real evil of the collective shadow acting here. The wheat and the weeds grow up together, lest in pulling up the weeds, one also pulls up the wheat.

In the midst of evil, being with God in prayer can be salvation from evil. One can recite a psalm in prison and find oneself as unafraid as in a verdant pasture. One can look prayerfully at a sunset on the way to one's execution, or prayerfully at one's executioner! Prayer is transendence and immanence. It is dealing with one's own, and with the collective shadow in all its externalizations, all its projections, head-on. Prayer is the acknowledgement of one's guilt in a context of infinite mercy. Praying is silence before the mystery of evil and, at the same time, hoping in the possibility of a solution to the great mystery of evil, which hope, in the end, is more important for living life than ever finding a solution. Translated into the language of the Christian mythological system, belief in the possibility of a solution would be the core of the Gospel: the coming of the Kingdom.

"Thy Kingdom come, thy will be done on earth as it is in heaven," Jesus prayed, looking out over the massive inconsistencies with that will in the society, in the religious leaders, in his friends, as well as in his enemies. Is our prayer, as his was, the active and contemplative transformation of those inconsistencies? Is "praying always" the harnessing of the conflicting energies of the will and the "non-will" for the growing of the Kingdom by working and doing, and by contemplating and transcendence? Is prayer both "time out" and "time in"; is prayer time spent building and time allowing to be built? The Kingdom needs to be built both within oneself and outside; one needs to remove the logs from one's own eye, know where one's own Shadow is before one can effectively transform the world. Is the stuff of the "time out" a gazing at a vision needed to direct the work of building? Is prayer, the contemplative kind of it, taking a look at the Architect's vision, so that the construction of his dream for oneself and the universe can move forward? Is contemplative prayer the letting be of the magnetism of the whole on the not whole, the unleashing of the force of the "already" on the "not yet"? In Christianity salvation is already accomplished, but not yet fulfilled. Christ has come but he will come again.

In an evolutionary world, perhaps, the Omega, the end time, the Kingdom, when God is all in all, has its teleological power of attraction on the fragmented diversity of the present, precisely at those points where God is most absent. In any case, in Judaeo-Christian theology, eschatology has always been the opening out of things to the "more." The future coming of the Messiah to Israel or the second coming of Christ for the Christian is the other pole to the historical salvation toward which we work. The shadows, the evil, the lacking, the incomplete, the imperfect, the darkness, the tears, the deaths will be met and banished by the "coming."

> Then I saw new heavens and a new earth. The former heavens and the former earth had passed away, and the sea was no longer. I also saw a new Jerusalem, the holy city coming down out of heaven from God, beautiful as a bride prepared to meet her husband. I heard a loud voice from the throne cry out, "This is God's dwelling among men. He shall dwell with them and they shall be his people and he shall be their God who is always with them. He shall wipe every tear from their eyes, and there shall be no more death or mourning, crying out or pain, for the former world has passed away." The One who sat on the throne said to me, "See, I make all things new!" Then he said, "Write these matters down, for the words are trustworthy and true!" He went on to say: "These words are already ful-

> filled! I am the Alpha and the Omega the Beginning and the End" (Rev 21:1–7a).

There is always danger of getting lost in this vision but there is a far greater danger in closing oneself off from this kind of a dream. Despair and bitterness immobilize. In the face of one's own evil shadow, pain, and death, confronted by the power of destruction and hell, one needs a coming.

There recently was a man buried alive in a mine cave-in, his whole body wedged in and immobilized by the debris surrounding him; only his head was able to move in a small pocket of space and air. The dream that there were those above who cared for him, who would move heaven and earth to reach and rescue him, was what kept him from going mad in the darkness. The faint hope that the sounds he heard were the sounds of a rescue operation gave him the energy to fight to stay conscious and alive, and eventually to be able to direct his rescuers by his voice calling out again and again.

At the same time that one needs this opening on to the rescuer God, this kind of a promise of a coming, this incessant calling out for the coming and exerting oneself to the limits of one's power to bring about the promise, one cannot lose sight of the reality of the evil of the collective shadow and the reality of the struggle against it. To establish the reality of evil as the polarity of the good, Jung went so far as to seem to posit evil or a shadow side of the divinity. In *Answer to Job*, he asks about the evil in the psychic image of God that so many people seem to experience and which Scripture seems to mirror. He questions the Yahweh who breaks three of his own commandments in his wager with Satan to test Job.[9] Jung points to the unconsciousness of Yahweh and the superior consciousness of Job. He claims that this sets the stage for the incarnation and that Job's answer comes when Jesus crucified calls out, "My God, my God why hast thou forsaken me?"[10] Here too he sees the struggle or opposition of God against God going on. Here, in Jesus, is God expecting to be saved from God by God as Job expected to be saved from God by God? Jung sees another example of the same thing in Jesus' teaching his followers to pray *to* the Father, "Lead us not into temptation."[11]

Jung's questions are very important because the psychic experiences they verbalize are very important. However, the questioning too is another example of the power of containment of evil by the

God myth. Jung takes the God myth seriously enough to question it as it struggles with the mystery of evil in each of the scriptural moments he cites. But even here evil projected on God is not absolutized but contained. Evil is contained by the consciousness of Job and of Jesus who in the midst of real evil truly expect a coming and hope for a solution. Evil is contained too in the followers who hope and pray in six petitions of the Lord's Prayer and in only one expect darkness and testing from him. The God myth holds while it never underestimates the power of evil. It is never naive about evil as the myth of the fall symbolizes so clearly:

> Evil is not symmetrical with the good; wickedness is not something that replaces the goodness of a man; it is the staining, the darkening, the defiguring of an innocence, a light and a beauty that remain. However radical evil may be, it cannot be as primordial as goodness.[12]

Jung's questioning highlights the opposing but tension-producing threads that run through Judaeo-Christian theology. There ran through the Hebrew Scriptures the tension of conditional and unconditional covenant, a universalism and a particularism, salvation for all and for the chosen. Christianity has as mentioned above an eschatology that is realized and unrealized; the Kingdom has come in Jesus but is not fulfilled. The great Christian tension exists between the Jesus of history and the Christ of faith and between the Christ and the whole Christ—head and members. The Christ of faith must always remain grounded in, and never be cut off from, the historical Jesus or Christianity becomes an ideology and not a relationship. At the same time the Christ event must always look toward ongoingness in history in the Spirit of Christ alive in those who are touched by that Spirit. The incarnation is ongoing in history. The place to look for God continues to be, as it was in Jesus, humanity itself.

III. Jesus and the Integration of the Shadow

Contemplating prayerfully the Jesus of history in whom the Christian believes God was living humanly is to look deeply into the fullest possibilities of being human. The emphasis of the humanity of Jesus which is a recovery made by contemporary Christology is a correction to an overemphasis on the divinity of Christ and a viewing of Christ solely from the perspective of his divinity. Theology had speculated on what was appropriate to God and then had predicated these same attributes of Jesus, effectively eliminating almost any trace of his being human in any true sense of the word. This Jesus could not be ill, could not grow in holiness, had exact foreknowledge of every event and enjoyed the Beatific Vision even from his cradle.

Critical Scripture studies distinguish a post-resurrectional perspective on the part of the authors of the Gospels. One needs to distinguish, in meditating on Jesus, these true but interpretive elements in which the first Christians tried to conceptualize and verbalize their extraordinary experiences of this person. If one can stand beside them in their encounters with Jesus, one can easily appreciate the beauty of the inspired mythologies that arose out of the primary process thinking of both Jesus and these early followers and which were preserved for us in the gems which comprise the New Testament. At the same time, if one can distinguish these mythologies, they need not obscure the true humanity of Jesus, nor the paradox he embodied.

Jung, who did not have the advantage of these twenty years of Christology, faulted the Christ symbol as missing the shadow, and so, as not being an altogether adequate symbol of the Self. Jung stated that "the Christ figure is not a totality, for it lacks the nocturnal side of the psyche's nature, the darkness of the spirit, and, also, is without sin."[13] In other words, if every psyche has a shadow how can the human psyche respond fully to this symbol. At the same time he did appreciate and refer to Christ as a symbol of the Self and regretted this "incompleteness."

It is certainly true to the whole of the text of the Gospels and to the affirmation of the whole Christian tradition to say that Jesus was without sin. However, "sin" is a theological term. It presumes God and a relationship to God and has no meaning if human actions, evil as well as good, have no ultimate significance. In other words, sin is an aberration of one's relationship with God. In Jungian terms this would also mean an aberration in one's relationship to one's Self, for Jung saw the God image as the symbol par excellence of the Self. In Jung's theory too, one can have a shadow and not surrender to it. In fact, in the movement toward wholeness one moves toward integrating one's shadow, not collapsing into it. For the most part the

Jesus we meet in the Gospels is an adult, well on his way toward wholeness, in fact manifesting from the very beginning an extraordinary movement to wholeness. Yet there is dynamism and movement and tension in every part of the Gospels. In the Christian story nevertheless, his death/resurrection is the culmination of that wholeness beyond our farthest dreams.

Perhaps we could imagine that the public life of Jesus is indeed the second half of his life. How early in his human development Jesus moved away from the kind of onesidedness that characterizes ego development in the first half of life can only be a matter of speculation. However, in the public life which is the subject of so much Christian prayer, we meditate on a Jesus who has made friends with his shadow, whether shadow as typology or taboo, potential for human growth or destruction. Perhaps Luke's story of the temptations is meant to summarize all the encounters of Jesus with his shadow in its most destructive guise. In the three temptations we see him confronted by the lures of humanity personified by Satan who seems to be outside, as he was in the poem about Job. He is tempted away from fidelity to Self and to God. He is perhaps being tempted to surrender to pleasure, power, and possessions: "Turn these stones into bread" (Lk 4:3); "Throw yourself down from here. . . . He will bid his angels watch over you" (Lk 4:9–10); "I will give you all this power and the glory of these kingdoms. . . . Prostrate yourself before me and it shall all be yours" (Lk 4:6–7). Perhaps the temptations are to ego worship or to inflation, since Jesus answers all of them by a reference to God. He will later state the fruit of this kind of experience in many paradoxical ways: "Whoever loses his life will keep it" (Lk 17:33); "Happy are the poor in spirit; the Kingdom of heaven is theirs" (Mt 5:3); "Happy are the single-hearted for they shall see God" (Mt 5:8).

It is important to see Jesus' statements as emanating from his own experience, from his own inner life, from his own reflection in prayer on his life experiences. Jesus was led into the desert by the Spirit. The desert is a place of solitude, the wasteland which has no value to society expect that it is a place of confrontation with one's Self. And God help the society that is confronted by a reformer who has never confronted the Self. It is a place where one is very conscious of the dependence of one's humanity on forces outside oneself. Food and water and shelter and the nourishment that comes from belonging, "being with" others, are all revealed in their stark necessity, here in their scarcity. The desert is a place where one is thrown back in the inner Self. The desert is a symbol of Christian spirituality for times of retreat and prayer. One goes into the desert to pray. "Out of the struggle of the desert comes the full grown spiritual man."[14] All the desert fathers tell of their struggles with evil spirits, forces most terrible and profound. The desert is the place to encounter the shadow with all its potential for both good and evil, growth and destruction. But the desert is the place where one finds God too. The desert can be a physical place but prayer can be such a desert too.

Jesus went into the desert to pray. He fasted for forty days and forty nights and he was hungry. He was vulnerable. He was face to face with all the poverty of his humanity but he was face to face too with the ultimate learning of his life: He was beloved Son in whom the Father was well pleased (Lk 3:22). In the desert, the whole Hebrew experience of God was very present to him. Luke has him quote Hebrew Scriptures as his own answers to the devil. Luke's story dramatizes Jesus' Self-confrontation. Were not the words of the devil the projection of promptings within Jesus to use his favor, his insight, his gifts, his power frivolously—"Turn these stones into bread . . . throw yourself . . . prostrate yourself"—so as to have whatever he wanted, to get things done and to do things the easy way? The favored and powerful always have the temptation to try to use their position or power to get what they want. To allow reality the freedom to be, or people to choose, is very difficult. Coercion is so much more efficient. Jesus had the vision of how things should be: the Kingdom. He had great genius and gifts to draw on. If only he could make it all happen now without having to win over and convince. Totalitarian dictatorships always seem so much more effective as a means to a utopia. Applying power and pressure is easier than motivating.

The rest of the Gospel can be read as Jesus' reply to the devil. Jesus has his power, he is aware of it, he knows its source as his unique kinship with the Father, but he doesn't use it to dominate. He shares it. He invites people into that power at its source: to recognize each his or her own unique relationship with God as Abba, each his or her own Kingdom within. The power of unique personhood flowing from an infinite source is an enormous potential. It is the reason for Self-love, a source of pride. One's power should be felt. One should make a difference in every circle one enters.

However, pride cut off from its source, or pride that takes to *itself,* the Source, is inflation and hubris. This pride would be an aberration of one's relationship with God, and one's Self, and, of course, with everyone else as well. This would be sin. Yet pride is a potential for good as well as evil. Jesus had the human energy, the shadow of pride. The devil in Luke's story put words in its mouth. The Jesus reflected in the four Gospels shows a wonderful integration of this energy of pride. He has an amazing sense of himself but always points to the Father as the Source of all he has and is. He is also at pains to point out the same possibilities and potentials within every other human person. Notice the Self-affirmation in: "I am the Way and the Truth and the Life; no one comes to the Father but through me" (Jn 14:5). And the affirmation of others in: "When *you* pray, say, Father" (Lk 11:2). In Matthew 5 he expresses his own sense of himself and his authority by repeating over and over, "You have heard the commandment . . . but what I say to you is. . . ." In contrast to this he says: "Put your trust *in God.* I solemnly assure you, whoever says to this mountain, Be lifted up and thrown into the sea, and has no inner doubts but believes that what he says will happen, shall have it done for him" (Mk 11:22–23). There is so much ambiguity and paradox in the Gospels because there is so much of it in Jesus who was so integrated. The words of Jesus as well as the actions of Jesus are filled with the kind of inconsistencies and contradictions that point to someone who is far from being onesided, one who has made friends with the shadow.

One can go through each of the capital sins and see how Jesus embodies the positive energy of each of them and calls his disciples to do so. Jesus shows us that in every vice there is some potential for good, just as in every virtue there is a potential for evil. That is why he praises the publican who is able to say: "Lord, be merciful to me a sinner" (Lk 18:13), while he berates the Pharisee who boasts of his virtue.

Jesus obviously enjoyed food and drink—so much so that he was accused of being a glutton and a drunkard while John the Baptist was an ascetic. Jesus tells his disciples not to fast while the Bridegroom is with them. He is constantly pictured as sharing meals with all sorts of friends and with sinners who were his friends, and talking about feasts and banquets. He even changes water into wine so a party can go on and newlyweds will not be embarrassed. He feeds the multitude with a superabundance. Yet he obviously *does not* live by bread alone. He is portrayed as being hungry and thirsty. He points to the birds of the air as a model of dependence on the Father who feeds them. He condemns the man who builds great barns to store his surplus grain and praises those who hunger and thirst for justice. He sends his disciples out provisionless, is himself dependent, and points to himself as food come down from heaven.

As with food and drink, Jesus obviously has an appreciation for all material things, even sometimes an awe of them, and above all covets people. The positive energies of the shadows of covetousness, envy, and lust are in him but integrated without the slightest trace of disorder. He sends the rich young man away to distribute all his goods to the poor but calls Matthew the dishonest tax collector to follow him. He chooses to eat in the house of the rich thief Zacchaeus and turns him into a generous philanthropist. He praises the woman who wastes the expensive perfume by pouring it on him. He appreciates the magnificence of the temple, the loaded fig trees, the heavy vines. He appreciates fine pearls, the pain of losing a coin, the value of a treasure found in a field. He sends the children of the Kingdom off to buy the field in question. He praises the craftiness and cunning of the unjust steward who can't dig and won't beg but acts on his plan to make friends by further cheating his master. Jesus is no naive innocent. He calls his followers to be as he was, wise as serpents and simple as doves.

He was not afraid of women or of affectivity. Love is central to his message and not anemic impersonal love. He exhibits a lust for life and, in the very best sense of the word, a lust for people. He surrounded himself with all kinds of men and women, all kinds of relationships, from warm one-time encounters to committed, intimate friendships. He is not afraid of, nor does he shun, human intimacy and demonstrations of affection. Martha and Mary, his close friends send him a message: "Lord, the one you love is ill" (Jn 11:3). John speaks of the beloved disciple who leans his head on Jesus' breast at the Last Supper. At least three times he is depicted as having his feet washed by a woman of questionable reputation. He will not uphold the law that the woman caught in adultery should be stoned. Only one who has made friends with his own shadow would say in such a setting: "Let the one who is without sin cast the first stone" (Jn 8:7).

At the same time, Jesus is depicted as unmarried, born of a virgin, questioning the relationship of the Samaritan woman with her five men, condemning adultery and easily dispensing with marriage bonds and even looking at another as an object of one's lust.

There is no doubt that Jesus was well aware of the evil that was within hearts, as well as the evil externalized in his society. He waged unceasing war on that evil and called his followers to fight injustice and pain and suffering caused by inequality and evil. There is no doubt that Jesus was appalled by the contrast between the goodness and love of God which he experienced and the massive evil and hatred he encountered.

The cross is the final paradox and the final reconciliation of these poles between which Jesus lived his life. He was finally torn apart by the unintegrated shadow energies and evil forces of his enemies. The power of that unintegrated shadow infected even his friends and followers who were helpless and hapless in the face of it. The cross of Jesus stands for all time as the sign of the result of unintegrated shadow. The execution and death of Jesus faces us from every steeple as a call to contemplation. The cross calls us to face our own shadows in prayer, in the containment and hope of his life and his resurrection. It is the hope that integration is possible to humanity, and that good comes out of evil. It is hope that out of my facing in prayer my own very real desires to live out the negative side of every one of the capital sins, I will not be overwhelmed but humanized. I will then be the last one to lynch or crucify someone else, for I will truly know that there but for the grace of God go I, or, better, there go I.

Notes

1. Ann and Barry Ulanov, *Primary Speech: A Psychology of Prayer* (Atlanta: John Knox Press, 1982), p. 2.
2. Joseph Campbell, *Myths To Live By* (New York: Bantam Books, 1973), p. 216.
3. *Ibid.*
4. Ann and Barry Ulanov, *Religion and the Unconscious* (Philadelphia: The Westminster Press, 1975), p. 27.
5. *Ibid.*
6. Strephon Kaplan Williams, *Jungian Senoi Dreamwork Manual* (Berkeley: Journey Press, 1980), p. 197.

7. John Welch, O. Carm., *Spiritual Pilgrims: Carl Jung and Teresa of Avila,* (New York: Paulist Press, 1982), p. 111.

8. John Sanford, *Evil: The Shadow Side of Reality* (New York: Crossroad, 1981), p. 40.

9. Carl G. Jung, *Answer to Job,* in *The Portable Jung,* ed. Joseph Campbell, trans. R.F.C. Hull (New York: Penguin, 1971), p. 539.

10. *Ibid.*, p. 576.

11. *Ibid.*, p. 529.

12. Paul Ricoeur, *The Symbolism of Evil* (Boston: Beacon Press, 1967), p. 156.

13. Carl G. Jung, Vol. 11: *Psychology of Religion: West and East, The Collected Works of C.G. Jung* (New Jersey: Princeton University Press, 1969), p. 232.

14. Kenneth Leech, *Soul Friend* (San Francisco: Harper and Row, 1980), p. 141.

CHAPTER 6

Toward a Definition of Play

I. Play and Maturity

The ability to play and be playful is a human possibility at all times and all ages. It is expressed in the behavior and life style of the truly mature person, from the three year old playing house, to the saint on the guillotine asking the executioner to be careful of his beard. A person can be mature at any age. We can have a mature two year old, sixteen year old, thirty, fifty, seventy-five, and ninety year old. If there is the possibility of maturity at all those ages, there is the possibility of immaturity. A person is mature at any age if the person is open to growth and development. The moment closure is made, a position of completion taken, immaturity takes over.

One of the very things which keeps us open to growth at every age is the ability to enter into play. Many people make a distinction between play and leisure. Here I am using them synonymously. When we speak of play, we may be using it as a verb, meaning a group of things one can engage in. Play can also be an adverb, describing an attitude one has about something one is doing or an attitude one has about one's whole life. Leisure can be a noun, meaning some part of one's day or life. It can also be an adjective, describing one's whole life, not just part of it, just as play can.

I want to discern the nature and purpose of play in adult life. I have already affirmed that the ability to play is integral to adult life and that one of the purposes of play is to help keep us open to growth and development. How do I understand "adult"? If I asked twenty different people when a person becomes an adult or what it means to be an adult, I could possibily get twenty different answers. Here are some possibilities. Adulthood is when you become economically independent, sexually active and capable of reproduction, legally accountable, eligible to vote, to bear arms, to drink. Adulthood is when you have reached the use of reason, are fully rational. Adulthood is having reached a certain age: seven, fourteen, eighteen, twenty-one. Adulthood is winning psychic independence from the primary adults who raised you. Adulthood is the state of being a mature person. People fumble for their answers, or they speak them dogmatically, and we remain dissatisfied and uneasy with all their responses. We not only have an uneasiness with the responses, we have an uneasiness over not being able to come up with what constitutes an adult.

This ambiguity reflects our own historical moment and the paradox inherent in adulthood. There is no doubt that our lifetime has been characterized by continual and profound turmoil and change, destructive and constructive. Culturally we have existed in a "no man's land," "on the boundary line," neither in the past cultural milieus, nor in the coming new culture. Our cultural milieu is neither "second wave" nor "third wave" style. We are living in the ferment of what was and what is to come. In this century we have witnessed a dramatic lengthening of the human lifespan. Even chronologically the adult years of a person have almost doubled. Our uneasiness with the attempts to define adult is in itself a good thing, for it points to the complexity of the matter. We have come to realize that being an adult is a paradox. It is a paradox because we grew up thinking that adult was the opposite of child, and today we have come to realize that "adult" incorporates, brings with it, the "child." We thought reaching maturity was a sign of adulthood, and now we have come to understand that maturity is the ideal state of every age.

In this, our new consciousness, we have moved beyond our Greek heritage that crowned reason and rationality as the highest of man's gifts (excluding children) as well as only a man's gift (excluding women). We have come to realize that adulthood does not consist in the possession of a faculty (reason) but in the process of becoming a human person. Of old, children and adults were exclusive of each other. Childhood was an inferior state. Today we see that childhood has its own beauty and integrity and that something of the child must be brought with the person through life. We carry the child with us through all our seasons: the season of youth, the season of mid-life and the season of the mature years. John Dunne reminds us that the whole person lies deep within us at every moment in all the seasons of life.[1]

> The child is there living with the unknown in the moment, playing as time itself plays with all the things of life in their seasons. The youth is there living with the unknown in his life, facing the things that must enter into his life. The man is there living with the unknown in death, facing the things

> of his life that must pass. The old man is there living with the unknown in his spirit. . . .[2]

William Bouwsma points out that in many ways childhood is a model for adulthood. Genuine adulthood merges with childhood in many areas, but none more poignantly than in play.[3] To be an adult we must maintain our ability to play and continually foster our own playful attitude toward life. We need to be diligent and serious about maintaining times for play and our playful attitude because the culture is not very supportive. Keeping play alive in us can become a game against the enemies of play within ourselves and against the culture that sees play as a child's thing. A game is a paradox in itself because it has a seriousness about it that keeps it interesting, stimulating, and playfully alive. If the adult keeps play alive in himself or herself long enough it will become a virtue, a way of life, integral to who he or she is as a person, as an adult. For such an adult play will be part and parcel of the rhythm of life as well as an attitude underlying all he or she does and the attitudes producing the rhythm of life itself. Alan McGlashan tells us that "rhythm is a mystery . . . the invisible wave on which Life itself is carried."[4] He reminds us of the two basic rhythms that we have, the heart beat which relates us to the whole of organic life, and the breathing which relates us to the life of the spirit.[5] The rhythm of play in our life is also deeply connected to our continual relationship to all organic life and our relationship to the events of our life and the significance of the events of our life, that is, the life of the spirit. Play allows us to be truly human, to live the rhythmic life, the life of the spirit.

In many of us a rhythm of play in our life seems to be prohibited by our commitment to our work, vocation, ministry. William A. Sadler warns us, "Our western disrespect for play as childish and unimportant may well be a symptom not of maturity but of cultural neurosis."[6] Play and work are two polarities that need to be incorporated in our whole society and in each individual. Our culture is at a turning point. Can it come to realize the potential good in each of these polarities for the individual and for the culture? We must have some individuals who need not wait for the culture to promote this balancing but can come to both values and tenaciously hold on to both polarities in the rhythm that promotes human life, the life of the spirit.

II. Play and Work

Work is a problem today. Many people don't have any work: children, older people, adolescents, the poor, unemployed adults. Work for many people is not creative. It does not flow from who and what they are. People are alienated from their work. There is a whole other group of people who are identified with their work. When asked "Who are you?" they respond, "A doctor," "a bishop," "a housewife," "an electrician," "a newspaper reporter," "a truck driver," etc. For another group of people, work is the sole source of their self-esteem and meaning.

For many people the book *The Three Boxes of Life* was an eye-opener. Bolles' thesis is that learning, working and playing (leisure) are the three major components of a person's lifetime and that the culture has unfortunately singled out the early years (5 to 22) for learning, the middle years (22–50) for working and the later years (50–68) for play (leisure). "That's the way it goes in our culture. . . . First an 'orgy' of learning, then an 'orgy' of working, and finally an 'orgy' of leisure."[7] The goal of his book is to help us envision, and move toward, a balance of working, playing and learning at whatever age we are. His aim is high—a balance of all three! One could see the need for including all three, but in a balance? If we want to act on this balancing in our own lifestyle planning (and I do believe it is a good idea) I suggest we had better do so playfully. Bolles points out that if someone in the middle stage of life (22–50) had no work, we would, undoubtedly, see it as a much graver situation than the person in the same stage who claimed that learning was not part of his life at all, or that leisure or play had no part in "his" life. I believe his point is well made. We have inflicted learning on our young people, work on the middle group and leisure on the later. We believe these cultural expectations will change only when enough individuals change, creating an integration of learning, working and playing in their own lives and the lives of those they touch and influence.

This is a major conversion in an individual's life as well as society's. Every individual has a need and a right to enter into the world of work, play and study. It appears basic that we do believe that all people are created equal and should enjoy their inalienable rights to life, liberty and the pursuit of happiness. Life, liberty and the pursuit of happiness require the right and opportunity to learning, to working and to playing. When a country has a large percentage of unemployment, people condemned to hours and hours of "leisure" because there is no work for them, this deprivation makes them not only unable to work but also unable to enter into authentic playing or learning. When the work someone is involved in does not flow from his uniqueness, is dull, monotonous, over-strenuous, and has simply an economic reward (whether that be high or puny), it stifles human creativity, spontaneity, sensitivity, awareness and growth. Once again we have a person not acclimated, not capable of the joys of genuine laughing or playing.

The absence of work for people is found both in the undeveloped countries and in our own highly-developed technological society. Late capitalism has gone through a global reconstruction that "entails the creation of an unemployable layer in society. In order to maintain the stability of society the state redirects part of the people's earnings through taxation and budgetary measures, to care for the section of the population that does not earn money."[8] The lack of humanization in such a society was evidenced in a recent block association meeting. Most of the members were blacks of the "poor working class" as they called themselves. One young black mother, the sole support of her two children, complained of the cutbacks the administration had leveled against her: "I hold down two jobs and go to school at night so I can make something of myself, and now I get no subsidy to help me with my two children. 'Quit your job and stay home,' they tell me, 'and you'll get a subsidy.' Yes, but will I get self-respect and will I get ahead and what about tomorrow?" I do not believe that this young woman has been given the rights to life, liberty and the pursuit of happiness. She is being denied the right to work, to learn and to play.

In such a society we cannot define work as what you must do and play as what you want to do, as some people define it. Nor can we define work, as still others wish to do, as the activity that gives me economic stability and play the activity for which I am not reimbursed. To talk of the relationship of play to adults and adult life I have to talk of the adult's total life condition. Is he or she an adult deprived of the right to work, like our young black mother or the fifty-five year old executive forced into retirement? Or is he an adult forced to work at a task that is dulling, uncreative, dehumanizing? I remember going on a tour of an assembly line production of a modern factory and being horrified at the thought of any person being submitted to that kind of work and that kind of environment. I was doubly horrified that it was being proudly shown off to the public as a model.

Is work that which provides us with a living wage? Or is work the human call and invitation to enter creatively into the process of living in a way for which we are most gifted and in which we can excel, thereby making our greatest contribution to our own living, the lives of others, this place, this world, this universe? One is inclined to build constructions, another to design them, still another to keep them in good order or to landscape them. Another is called to make laws, to enforce laws, another to tend sheep, another to provide the far places with foods grown on the farms, another to canning, forestry, creative problem-solving, large-city sanitation, teaching, providing others with the pleasure of music, presenting the population with the news, recording history, theologizing on life-experiences, preaching the word of God, practicing medicine, caring for the dying, publishing books, typing manuscripts, holding public office, providing telephone service, entertaining people, scientific research, finding creative ways to feed the multitude, giving child care, exploring space, searching for new sources of energy, providing police protection, discovering a modern diplomacy, translating languages, and on and on. The modern day life of a person, country, the world demands a multitude of known and yet-to-be-discovered tasks to create a harmonious and progressively more and more human life style. The humanization of work is badly needed. The person's right to work, to enter into making a personal and a creative contribution to society and to be able to provide for his or her own needs economically, is a human right and need.

Alvin Toffler recognizes that the world we grew up in, "the second wave," was accompanied by the spread of the Protestant work-ethic. The work-ethic highlighted thrift, increasing toil and the deferral of gratification. The "Puritan" characterizes all three traits. The ability to be thrifty at times, to toil untiringly when necessary and to defer gratification when desirable are all important human capabilities, I agree, but so are their opposites: to give and spend lavishly, to take genuine rest and leisure and to experience fully and with the deepest satisfaction. The growing increase of the use of drugs to induce a pleasurable experience and reduce the stress of boredom, of monotony and of conflict is a sign of how many people do not know how to avail themselves of the natural pleasures and ecstatic experiences of life. Our neurotic suppression of our deep human need for a sense of fulfillment and gratification, and our inability to deal with this need, leads many to solve their problems with the instant gratification of drugs. As we need work that is humanizing, we need play that is also humanizing.

Economic development and work are not the be-all and end-all of everything. Recently we were reminded that work is for humanity, not humanity for work. It is Toffler's hypothesis that our civilization is on the brink of the "third wave." And how does he describe people in the new civilization?

> Above all, they seem likely to crave balance in their lives—balance between work and play, between production and consumption, between headwork and handwork, between the abstract and the concrete, between objectivity and subjectivity.[9]

Toffler is not envisioning a utopian person, just a more human person. He believes that individuals will vary more vividly tomorrow, each living out his or her own uniqueness. He envisions that they will grow up sooner and show responsibility at an earlier age. This would surely be the result if the early years moved more toward a balance of work, play and learning! People in the new civilization will resist working for money alone.[10] Their work will flow from who they really are, their giftedness, and will be seen as service. Much of their time will be spent in filial community, in creative home making. Pleasure will be more simple and earthy, not dependent on consumerism. In such an atmosphere all will tend to a more global attitude in living, enjoying and safeguarding life as part of a global community.

We realize more and more that people of our generation as a whole are deprived of the joy of working in something that they are truly suited for and are burdened by a duality between person as worker and person as player. The human person has the need and ability of throwing himself or herself into the journey and adventure of living by the inherent ability and desire to work and to play. Play is absent from adult life because it is seen as a childish thing and not compatible with a serious, industrious nature. Play is seen as the opposite of work, incompatible with the same cause or intention, rather than as a complementary activity creating a rhythmic flow of energy, interest and absorption and harmoniously fulfilling the human spirit.

III. Play, Growth, Well-Being

Abraham Maslow showed us that the ability to play was one of the ideal traits of the human personality that he characterizes as "self-actuated." In an attempt to come to understand two of the most wonderful people he ever met, two of his own teachers, Maslow came to his theory of "self-actualization." It disclosed a common pattern or syndrome of growth among older people who have already lived much of their lives and were visibly successful, healthy, strong, creative, saintly and sagacious. He found that such people devote themselves to some cause outside themselves and all are found to have pursued and held tenaciously onto a common set of personal values which Maslow coined the "being values." These values were: truth, goodness, beauty, wholeness, dichotomy-transcendence, aliveness, uniqueness, perfection, necessity, completion, justice, order, simplicity, richness, effortlessness, playfulness, self-sufficiency.[11] According to Maslow, a fully human person is one tending toward these values and experiencing them in the numerous peak moments of life. He goes on to further describe playfulness as fun, joy, amusement, gaiety, humor, exuberance and effortlessness.[12] In this sense playfulness appears to be an attitude. There is a reciprocal relationship between our having special times for play in our day, week, month, year and our having a playful attitude in all we do and in life itself. Having time for play, making it an integral part of our life, essential to the rhythmic flow of our living, preserves a spirit of play in all we do. At the same time our spirit of play helps us to preserve a time for play in the rhythm of our life.

It appears that play is not only essential for psychological wholeness, but physical wellness too. The cardiologists Friedman and Rosenman tell us that some adults

> lack interest in the broader satisfaction of life and human culture. Those activities which are generally considered human and edifying—the great works and achievements in

> art, music, drama, philosophy, history, science, and indeed the charms of nature itself—only too often tend to bore him. This sort of person eventually becomes so caught up in the process of acquiring more and more things in less and less time that he has little desire or need to interest himself in any other intellectual or spiritual process. . . . You are rapidly dehumanizing yourself and in a most dangerous manner. What will there be left of your personality in a few short years if this spoilage continues unchecked? In a very real way, you are buying your way through life by selling yourself?[13]

These doctors discerned a certain pattern of behavior, a syndrome or "action-emotion complex," held in common by almost all of their patients. They believed that such people were trading themselves in for money, or whatever cause they were spending themselves on. In reality, they saw such people as killing themselves. They advise "Type A" people, as they called them, how to go about changing the death killing pattern of behavior characterized by hurry sickness and an excessive competitive spirit:

> Set aside a portion of each day for pursuits that have nothing to do with your normal vocation. Use this time to expand your fields of interest and enjoyment. The subject matter is less important than your attitude toward it; the critical point is that you somehow detach yourself from the narrow pattern of work and short-circuited emotion. . . . How long has it been since you noticed yourself warming to someone new, how long since you made even the mildest effort to bring a new person into your life and affections? . . . Another form of emotional sustenance crucial to the reviving personality is a stock of fulfilling and pleasant memories. You must make a very conscious effort each day to choose from among the passing events and experiences those which yield pleasure. Enjoy them as you live through them; indeed, concentrate on savoring them. . . . What your personality needs is latitude—for fantasies, dreams, fresh hopes. Only you can provide it. In short you are being urged to inject "unexpectedness" into your life if only because it is the key element of true humanity.[14]

Friedman and Rosenman are actually saying that adults who concentrate on their economic, professional or vocational life with all their time and emotional, psychic energy are less than human. They have neglected their own human ability and need to be engaged in something other than work. They have become myopic. They have critically limited themselves, denying whole other areas of their personality, bringing physical and emotional havoc. Perhaps one will not succumb to illness, to death, during one's working career years, but how prepared is this man or woman for retirement, for the years that are an invitation to self-fulfillment and spiritual growth?

> The identification of adulthood with the strong, rational, productive individual hits older men the hardest! White men in United States' society do not on the average live much beyond "retirement age." They seem to sense the logic that if to be a man is to be a worker, then to retire is to cease to be a man.[15]

We all have a need to be open and attentive to the natural, intellectual and artistic wonders that abound—offering both stimulation and pleasure. When we don't, we deprive ourselves of the abundant energy that comes from living through and stirring up a wealth of moments of deep satisfaction and pleasure. I dare say the same characteristics of the potential coronary victim are the characteristics of the atrophied adult, the one who is not on the way to "self-actualization" or "self-fulfillment."

If a psychiatrist or counselor sees that his or her patients or counsellees can laugh at some of the ridiculous manifestations of their own behavior or thoughts, he or she is heartened. Laughter can often be a sign of wellness. Norman Cousins discovered that it can be a cure for illness. Healing is a mystery. It is also an art. The doctor practices medicine. He enters into the art of his profession. The patient too enters into the healing of the body, mind and spirit. The doctor collaborates with the patient in the art of healing. When Norman Cousins took sick with a serious collagen disease in 1964 he turned to the wisdom figure within himself to discern the cure for his illness. He was fortunate to have a physician who was not threatened by this attitude of his patient. Surveying his past history, Norman came to believe that he had suffered a case of adrenal exhaustion while engaged in intensive work. He recalled reading that adrenal exhaustion was caused by emotional tension such as frustration or suppressed rage. Then the insight came to him:

> What about the positive emotions? If negative emotions produce negative chemical changes in the body, wouldn't the positive emotions produce positive chemical changes? Is it possible that love, hope, faith, laughter, confidence, and the will to live have therapeutic value? Do chemical changes occur only on the downside?[16]

With his doctor's approval, Norman checked himself out of the hospital and began a regimen of exercising affirmative emotions in order to change his body chemistry and effect a natural cure for himself. He found it easy to engage in faith, hope and love, but laughter was another matter. He engaged in viewing old-time movies. In his own words,

> It worked. I made the joyous discovery that ten minutes of genuine belly laughter had an anesthetic effect and would give me at least two hours of pain-free sleep. When the pain-killing effect of the laughter wore off, we would switch on the motion picture projector again, and, not infrequently, it would lead to another pain-free sleep interval.[17]

This laughter medicine proved, for Norman, that laughter as medicine had a physiological basis. In his case laughter was the regenerative force that brought about the restoration of his health despite the fact that specialists told him his disease was progressive and incurable. Patricia Flynn reminds us that "the Greek philosopher Democritus believed that our minds were given to us to turn the tragedy of life into a comedy."[18] Cousins is another witness to our need to build in times for laughter and fun. A rhythm of laughter and fun running through our days will temper our single-minded seriousness and put us on the way to better well-being. Play and laughter are not only instruments of healing, they are also preventive medicine of physical, emotional and spiritual sickness. Playing is a natural and human way of being in the world that engenders a new consciousness fostering individual and communual well-being. Playing is part of the art of living. It is a genuine sign of faith, hope and love. It is the natural response of the mature individual at any age that has profound ramifications on the total person.

IV. Play and the Individual

What experiences of play did you have in your childhood? List them.

Were they alone or with others?

Were they active or passive play?

How did they affect you?

Which were the most enjoyable to you? Why?

Are there any play experiences of childhood that you particularly cherish? Why?

Were any of your play experiences unhappy ones? Why?

Were there any play experiences of your childhood that still are things that you could, or do, thoroughly enjoy today?

As an adult, did you reach a time when you stopped playing? When? Why?

Think back. What was the most enjoyable moment or evening that you had in the past week? month? year?

What is the most enjoyable part of each day for you?

What kind of things do you most enjoy doing? Which are things you do alone? Which with others?

Are any free—cost nothing?

Look at your typical day, month, year. How much time is given to work, study, leisure or play?

When was the last time you were really surprised? When did you last surprise someone else?

Name the people you enjoy spending time with. Can you tell why? Do these people know that you enjoy being with them? When was the last time you were with each of these people?

Most of us have five priceless jewels that can be the source of deep pleasure, satisfaction, relaxation and vitality. How has each been that to you in the past? (SEE, SMELL, TOUCH, TASTE, HEAR)

Imagine and describe a perfect day when you consciously used all your senses to receive the pleasure and enjoyment that they can be a source of.

How can you move to make each day a little more like your imaginary day?

It is only in play that we are able to see and experience whole other areas of self, our personality. Play is like a friend. It makes you know that you are valuable for something other than your work and accomplishments. Play, like a friend, delights in you and lets you delight in yourself and someone else. Play, like a friend, never uses you. Play is like a friend because it changes your consciousness and relativizes that which you go about so seriously each day. As a friend can transform us and our situation, so can play. A friend can help us to put distance between ourselves and a situation in which we are emotionally involved; so too can play. A friend can help us to objectify our standpoint and see something from a new perspective; so too can play. A friend helps us to see another person's point of view, another person's experience, another way of doing things, so too does play. A friend demands our emotional energy and concern, thus taking us away from the busyness of our lives; so too does play. A friend fosters our personal development in areas we would not have chosen; so too does play. A friend encourages us to see new possibilities, embark on new adventures; so too does play. A friend brings us to greater awareness of ourselves, helps us to accept the parts of ourselves that we despise or do not cherish; so too does play. A friend is someone we always have; though time may pass, distance come between us, and new friends come along, the old friend is always part of the fabric of who we are; so too are all our genuine play experiences.

"To live creatively means first of all to play. In playing [one] becomes liberated from conditioning forces and learns to be open so as to discover the most important possibilities in life. Play as a source of our creativity is the pathway to the most meaningful dimensions of human freedom."[19] Play, like a friend, is most personal to who we are. I remember a grand old man, talking about experiences that refreshed and energized people, saying, "Don't tell me to go for a walk in the woods; just let me out to the horse races." The questions at the start of this section were to encourage each of us to pursue a deeper knowledge of ourself and what kinds of play we each enjoy. Some of our play experiences may be new to the stage of life we are in, and other play experiences may have followed us through life's stages. As a child I always loved playing with the earth, smelling it, feeling it. For a long period of time I deprived myself of this refreshment. Only recently, lying in the leaves on an autumn day, did I realize that one of my greatest pleasures and relaxations was right at my fingertips—toes! As a child on the beach I remember being puzzled by the adults who spent as much time lying on the beach as I did being in the water. I would swim and play until my teeth chattered, lips turned blue and "goose pimples" appeared. Today I love to lie on the beach, drink in the beauty of the ocean, listen to the sounds of the surf, feel the rays of the sun, taste the salt air, allow the beach aroma to fill me as I relax in this great wealth and passively watch the children at play. The earth and the sea still have a fascination for me though it may appear that my response to both has changed. Both call me to play in an enticing way. "Why?" I ask myself. "For by contacting Mother Earth, nature in us can be restored. We are put once more into touch with our natural selves, and a state of both physical and psychological health is regained. Most people have experienced the healing effect of stretching out on the ground in the woods or by the sea when they are tired or depressed. It is as if in this way our connection with the source of life is re-established and we get back into a right relation with Nature."[20]

Personality type has much to do with play. One's attitude toward life, extroversion or introversion, has a great deal to do with what is genuine play for each of us. Most extroverts have a great need for sociability because they are energized, turned on, by people. "Talking to people, playing with people, and working with people is what charges their battery."[21] The opposite is true of most introverts. They are not energized by people, but drained, worn out by them. They can be very sociable and effective ministers giving their all to others in whatever profession they are in. They can interact with people at great depth, but will be drained by the experience and need a time out, alone, to be refreshed. This would be true in a social, play or working situation. "The introvert is not a party pooper; he is pooped by the party."[22]

Understanding your patterns of play in childhood and young adulthood in terms of your attitude of introversion or extroversion may help you to seek the play that is most satisfactory to you, comes from you, despite what others think or say. At the same time we should encourage ourselves to be adventurous and enter into something new and different. In the second half of life the attitude that has not been our favorite, representing whole other unconscious parts of ourselves not yet developed, tends to be freed and have its part in our personality. Introverts may find themselves inclined to more extroverted play activities and extroverts may find themselves desirous of playtime alone or the pursuit of a more interior, solitary kind of pleasure. We must then provide ourselves with the kinds of play and pleasure that are truly our own and yet be open. Having a good friend with the opposite attitude from yours can do much to teach you to develop other parts of yourself and enjoy play of another kind.

Kiersey and Bates tell us that "J's" (*J*udging-type personalities) seem to all have a work ethic that makes them put work before everything else, while "P's" (*P*erceptive-type people) have a play ethic demanding that the work itself be enjoyable. A "J" would demand that the work be finished before the "J" could play, while the "P" would leave the work to enter into play or rest. In this case "P's" would find it easier building in play as part of the rhythm of their day, while "J's" will find it very difficult, especially in the first half of life. In the second half of life the absolute need of time out for play and a playful attitude toward life will push them to achieve a repatterning, to be converted. You know you are a judging type or a perceiving type by seeing which of your two favorite functions is extroverted. You are a "J" if you use your judgment function to deal with the outer world and a "P" if you use your perceptive function to deal with the outer world. Judging people close off perception quickly and come to quick decisions or judgments. Perceptive people delay or shut off judgment and remain open, looking for new evidence or developments. "This preference makes the difference between the judging people, who order their lives, and the perceptive people, who just live them."[23]

If you are an extroverted person your primary function is extroverted and your auxiliary is introverted. That is, you deal with the outside world with your primary function and your inner world with your auxiliary. If you are introverted, your primary function is introverted and your secondary function is extroverted. The basis of this typology comes from the theory of Carl Jung. In his book *Psychological Types* he elaborates on his theory that each of us has four functions, two that are perceptive and two that are judging, and that each of us makes an unconscious choice to favor one over the other. We perceive things through our intuition and senses. We make our judgments with our feelings and our thinking. One of each pair constitute the two functions that you have developed. Each of us has developed a perceiving and a judging function. The other functions are undeveloped within us. Of your two developed functions, one is primary, your overall favorite, and the other is your auxiliary or secondary function. It was Isabel Briggs who added to Jung's typology the dimension of being a perceptive or judging type, thus creating a fourth pair of opposites to Jung's three: introvert/extrovert, sensing/intuition, and thinking/feeling. The four pairs are evidenced in the Myers-Briggs Personalilty Survey, while another popular typology indicator, the Gray-Wheelwright, only determines Jung's original three.

If you know your attitude (introvert or extrovert) and your primary and auxiliary function, you can discern whether your fourth aptitude is judging or perceiving. Whichever of your functions is extroverted tells you whether you are a perceptive or a judging type. If you are extroverted and your primary function is thinking or feeling, you are a judging type. If you are an extrovert and your primary function is intuition or sensing, you are a perceiving type. Because it is the introvert's secondary function that is extroverted, her type is determined by this auxiliary. If the introvert's auxiliary is thinking or feeling, she is a judging type. If the introvert's auxiliary is intuition or sensing, she is a perceptive type.

The mid-life transition is an invitation to accept both the strengths of our personality and the means of play that are particularly our own because of our typology. At the same time we must realize that the undeveloped are also true parts of ourselves, foster their development and the corresponding enjoyment and means of play they can provide for us. It could well be that our unconscious, undeveloped personality can be the source of our greatest pleasure, creativity and delights in the second half of life. In my own case, being an intuitive, contacting the earth and the sea, allows me to experience my least developed or inferior function, sensing.

Kiersey and Bates point out discoveries about the types and their characteristic relationship to work and play. They discerned that the sixteen Jungian types fell into four classifications and they named each of the four after a Greek god: Apollo, Dionysius, Prometheus and Epimetheus.[24] The Dionysians are characterized by the joy they have and give to others. They are hungry for freedom and have a need for independence. For those types of very active people, all work is essentially play. They go about their work in the same spirit and style as they do play. Friends think of them as fun to be with and the kind of people that lift your spirit with a contagious optimism and excitement. These Dionysians are all perceptive types whose extroverted function is sensing. The sensing perceptive types that are Dionysians are: introverted thinkers whose auxiliary is *sensing*, introverted feelers whose auxiliary is *sensing*, extrovert *sensing* with thinking as the auxiliary, and extrovert *sensing* with feeling as auxiliary. All four types (ISTP, ISFP, ESTP, ESFP) tend to live for today and enjoyment is uppermost in their mind because it is a need for them. These are the people, I believe, who must truly have lived a crucifixion in the Puritan colonies because their typology was so much opposed to all the Puritans stood for.

The Epimethean temperament was more suited for a Puritan colony. They have the real work-ethic. If the Dionysian gives us joy, the Epimethean gives us a sense of duty. Social status is most important for them as it gives them a clear sense of roles and reciprocal duties and responsibilities. They have a real need to always be useful and to serve. As much as the Epimethean can give to and care for others, they have difficulty receiving and being cared for. As the Dionysian is an optimist, the Epimethean is a pessimist. Quick to work, he is slow to play if he plays at all. He gives lavishly in time and zeal for work, but in all areas spends almost nothing because of an inbuilt thrift and conservation. Although Epimetheans are hungry for a sense of belonging, they are quick to condemn the non-traditionalist, taboo-breakers and non-conformists. Because work is their ethic, play has little meaning for their lives. This type, all "J's" characterized by their work-ethic, are the Introverts whose primary function is sensing with either *feeling* or *thinking* as an auxiliary, and the Extroverts whose auxiliary function is sensing with a primary function of either *feeling* or *thinking* (ISFJ, ISTJ, ESFJ, ESTJ). These initials given are as in the Myers-Briggs Indicator and they give in sequence the attitude, perceptive function, judging function, and the perceptive or judging attitude.

Now there is a type that finds genuine play almost impossible, not because they have a work-ethic like the Epimetheans, but because they go about playing in the same way that they go about working. These are the people who have both thinking and intuition as their functions despite their position as primary or secondary: introverted thinkers with intuition as the auxiliary, introverted intuitives with thinking as an auxiliary, extrovert thinking with intuition as an auxiliary, extrovert intuitive with thinking as an auxiliary. This group plays and has a good time because they know it is the right thing to do. This makes all their play to be work. In reality they are using the same parts of their personality playing as they do working. They have a need to understand everything and are noted for intelligence and competence. These Prometheans live in and for their work (INTJ, INTP, ENTP, ENTJ).

All those whose conscious personality is characterized by intuition and feeling, despite which one is primary or auxiliary, are the goal-oriented Apollonians. Noted for the spirit that engulfs them and which they pass on to others, their type is in constant search for fulfillment, self-actualization and unity for themselves and others. They are in quest of meaning and the significance of everything. This type has a need to be engaged in work that is meaningful. They find it difficult to desert their search for meaning, to play. Because they tend to make total commitments and find it difficult to limit themselves, they also find it hard to leave behind their quest and play and relax. Never limiting the time and energy that they devote to their cause affects their willingness to give time and energy to playing. These are the introvert intuitives with feeling as an auxiliary, introvert feelers with intuition as an auxiliary, extrovert feelers with intuition as an auxiliary, and extrovert intuitives with feeling as an auxiliary (INFJ, INFP, ENFJ, ENFP). The Apollonians are like Apollo who had a mission to bring peace and happiness to people. This is the goal of all their work and their play.

When I studied these four types named after the Greek gods that Kiersey and Bates give us I quickly came to see that only one of the four classifications is noted for a spirit of play. This means that only four of Jung's sixteen types are noted for a spirit of play. The Dionysians have a felt need for joy and playing, while the Epimetheans have a felt need for work because it is their duty to serve others, the Prometheans for work because they have a felt sense to understand and control things, the Apollonians for work because they have a felt sense of a mission to give others meaning and spirit. For only one out of four types, therefore, will genuine play be consistently actualized in the first half of life. The Myers reflect what Kiersey and Bates say about Dionysians when they describe sensing types: "Face life observantly, craving enjoyment. . . . Are by nature pleasure lovers and consumers; loving life as it is and having a great capacity for enjoyment, they are in general contented. . . . Contribute to the public welfare by their support of every form of enjoyment, recreation, and every variety of comfort, luxury and beauty."[25] This description of sensing types sounds like a description of the Dionysians that are characterized by extroverted sensing being all perceptive types.

Because the second half of life is a call to transform (not change) our personality type and to develop the other functions and the opposite attitude, there is a genuine possibility that the mid-life transition will effect a conversion in regard to play. People in mid-life, open to growth and change, will begin to have a felt sense for things other than what has been their primary concern. They will begin to feel their own lack of development, lack of wholeness, joyfulness, spontaneity and expansiveness. This is a summons to us to give attention to our neglected functions and attitude. They are part of our shadow. They are the hidden unconscious side of our personalilty that we see as inferior and unfavorable. Now as our values are shifting we too are inclined to see within ourselves what we once repressed, unconsciously. Now these aspects of our shadow can be a creative source to the development of our personality. They can become the source of unexpected joy and delight. In mid-life onesidedness becomes more and more a curse and there is an invitation to wholeness or inviduation As this movement progresses in us, we who have not developed our human ability to play, nor a playful rhythm of life, have hopes that this will be the outcome of our second journey. Perhaps some friends will someday say of us what Laurens van der Post said of Carl Jung (he only knew Jung in Jung's later life),"No one made me laugh as much as he made me laugh . . . he was a man of great energy and good humor."[26] I believe that adults who successfully negotiate a mid-life transition experience in their later years a new strength, power and wisdom. Is it possible that at the heart of this final Pentecost in a person's life is the true pearl of great price, a spirit of play?

Notes

1. John S. Dunne, *Time and Myth* (New York: Doubleday, 1973; University of Notre Dame Press edition, 1975), p. 127.

2. *Ibid.*, p. 128

3. William J. Bouwsma, "Christian Adulthood," *Adulthood*, edited by H. Erickson (New York: W.W. Norton Co., 1978), p. 88.
4. Alan McGlashan, *Gravity and Levity* (Boston: Houghton Mifflin Co., 1976), p. 123.
5. *Ibid.*, p. 135.
6. William A. Sadler, Jr., "Creative Existence," *Humanitas* (Personality and Play), Vol. 5, No. 1, p. 58.
7. Richard N. Bolles, *The Three Boxes of Life* (Berkeley: Ten Speed Press, 1978), p. 335.
8. Ivan Varga, "Capitalism and the Return to Religion," *The Ecumenist* (May–June 1980), p. 55.
9. Alvin Toffler, *The Third Wave* (New York: William Morrow, 1979; Bantam Edition, 1981), p. 391.
10. *Ibid.*
11. Abraham H. Maslow, *Religious Values and Peak Experiences* (New York: Viking Press, 1970; 5th printing, 1972), pp. 92–94.
12. *Ibid.*, p. 94.
13. Meyer Friedman, M.D., and Ray H. Rosenman, M.D., *Type A Behavior and Your Heart* (Connecticut: Fawcett Publications, paperback ed., 1974), p. 221.
14. *Ibid.*, pp. 222–223.
15. Gabriel Moran, *Education Toward Adulthood* (New York: Paulist Press, 1979), p. 28.
16. Norman Cousins, "Anatomy of an Illness (As Perceived by the Patient)," in *The Healing Continuum*, ed. Patricia Anne Randolph Flynn (Maryland: Robert J. Brady Co., a Prentice-Hall Publishing, 1980), p. 378.
17. *Ibid.*, p. 381.
18. Patricia Anne Randolph Flynn, *Holistic Health* (Maryland: Robert J. Brady Co., a Prentice-Hall Publishing, 1980), p. 187.
19. William A. Sadler, Jr., "Creative Existence: Play as a Pathway to Personal Freedom and Community," *Humanitas*, Vol. 5: Personality and Play (Spring 1969), p. 73.
20. M. Esther Harding, *The I and the Not I* (Princeton, N.J.: Princeton University Press, 1965; Bollingen Paperback ed., 1973), p. 40.
21. David Kiersey and Marilyn Bates, *Please Understand Me* (Del Mar, California: Prometheus House, 1978), p. 14.
22. *Ibid.*, p. 15.

23. Isabel Briggs Myers and Peter B. Myers, *Gifts Differing* (Palo Alto, California: Consulting Psychologist Press, 1980), p. 9.

24. Kiersey and Bates, *Please Understand Me*, pp. 27–66.

25. Isabel Briggs Myers and Peter B. Myers, *Gifts Differing*, p. 63.

26. B.B.C. television documentary, "The Story of Carl Gustav Jung," Jonathan Stendall producer, filmed in 1971.

CHAPTER 7

Individuation and Play

I. Play and the Second Half of Life

A. *I put on Beethoven's Ninth Symphony and picked up one of the two dozen books that surrounded me. I was in the midst of researching this very topic. Something urged me to put the book down. The music beckoned to me inviting me to come and play. In a short time I had relinquished the pressing task. I was no longer the student searching. I was not the minister responsible for discovering and uncovering the insight that will touch. I was not driven to complete the work I was intuitively called to. I was that other carefree person delighting in the music that lifted me up, carried me with it. For the length of the symphony I had no pressing goals, no zeal for knowledge, no anxiety. I was beyond all that. I was in delight.*

B. *It was a hot summer night. The forty-five minute drive from the office in the stop and go traffic put distance between the affairs at work and the affairs at home. At home there was the domestic scene: a meal to cook, the conflict and nurturing of personal relationships to tend to, an aging depressed father, noisy bothersome tenants, adult children struggling to be free. But first there was this ritual of going right down to the beach for a swim before engaging in the evening activities. They grew accustomed to these moments of play. They looked forward to the walk to the ocean, the race into the water, the luxury of those waves, the enticing salt water warmed by the day's sun. Here they were children again, or just lovers and playmates. For these too few minutes this man and woman had freedom from life's demands, life's goals.*

C. *They each delighted in jogging. Every morning they met at six despite the weather and jogged. Most times not a word was spoken. A clap on the back, just a smile or nod, at most a brief word or two and they started out, all five of them. Every interest, every concern, every serious situation was relinquished as they let their body take over and they surrendered themselves to this experience. Each one found himself to be more than his concern, his adult preoccupation, the demands made upon him, his failures and successes. Here the body took over and the spirit surged in freedom. And for each of them there was a communal experience of being with others in this special way. They experienced a spiritual support that was a "felt sense" as they ran side by side, as they played in the early morning a play that was strangely life giving, a playing that was a lifting, a soaring of the body, mind and heart.*

All of us in the second half of life can pay heed to Carl Gustav Jung's counsel and advice to his friend Father Victor White, "Don't work too much."[1] Our three vignettes are only samples of the numerous ways people in mid-life years and beyond are called to engage in play. As our lives unfold during these years we express ourselves in the work we do, the many levels of relating that we engage in, and in the life of the spirit expressed and found in the rhythm of playing and praying built into our lives as well as underpinning all we do. Play is and must be part of the way we spend our time as well as the attitude that describes the very art of living. It takes the four seasons of our life to become a whole person. It takes the four seasons of our life to develop the art of doing all things playfully; that is, religiously.

Our ability to play, to let go of our ego centered lives, to move away from our conscious goals, is crucial to the developmental tasks of the second half of life, individuation. Individuation calls for a change of dominance. The ego or conscious self must be diminished so that the unconscious personality can come to realization. This meshing of the conscious and unconscious personality gives rise to the Self. More and more, as we move through the second half of life, the Self becomes the all-important realization. It is our very ego strengths that allow us to enter into altered states of consciousness in both playing and praying. In play we let go of the consciousness that directs our energies and we experience whole other areas of our being. Our unconscious encounters us in these moments and we experience the miracle of transcending conflicting values and opposites. In play all things are possible and all things can work together for the good.

As we move through the transition from the first half of life to the second we are called to relax, to cease our terrible serious-mindedness, to encounter our unconscious, our hidden Self. We are weary from the busy tasks and engagements of the first half of life. In our weariness we find it difficult to settle down,to listen to our own organism, to experience the movement within. We are prone to a holy activity, busyness and noise. Anne Morrow Lindberg describes her encounter with the sea, and it is a striking description of a person in mid-life encountering her unconscious, the other half of her personality and the seedlings of her true Self. Listen to this woman at play on the beach.

> At first the tired body takes over completely. As on shipboard, one descends into a deck-chair apathy. One is forced against one's mind, against all tidy resolutions, back into the primeval rhythms of the sea-shore. Rollers on the beach, wind in the pines, the slow flapping of herons across sand dunes, drown out the hectic rhythms of city and suburb, time tables and schedules. One falls under their spell, relaxes, stretches out prone. One becomes, in fact, like the element on which one lies, flattened by the sea; bare, open, empty as the beach, erased by today's tides of all yesterday's scribblings.
>
> And then, some morning in the second week, the mind wakes, comes to life again. Not in a city sense—no—but beach-wise. It begins to drift, to play, to turn over in gentle careless rolls like those waves on the beach. One never knows what chance treasures these easy unconscious rollers may toss us, on the smooth white sand of the conscious mind; what perfectly rounded stone, what rare shell from the ocean floor. . . . One should lie empty, open, choiceless as a beach—waiting for a gift from the sea.[2]

Here in the unique depths of solitary play, Anne Morrow Lindberg is open to experience other dimensions of herself. She knows that these breakthroughs of the unconscious are gifts to be integrated into her image of herself. Be it soliltary play, the playful companioning of friends in moments of intimacy, or the freedom and joy of individuals at play in a social milieu, all are experiencing other dimensions of Self. It is this very experience that is at the heart and core of the process of individuation.

Individuation is the process of personality growth in the second half of life. A woman born in the United States in 1970 can expect to live to 75.6 years. A woman born here in 1985 can expect to live to 78.3 years. The increased life span of the human person has placed greater emphasis on life beyond forty. The experience of individuals and the scientific study of the life span and personality development points to the continued growth of personality in the mid-years and old age, the mature season of one's life. We have always considered death before forty to be premature, as well as death in the decade of the forties, fifties, or even sixties. In Jewish-Christian tradition a long life has been considered a blessing and worthy of being asked for in prayer. Consider the Sacred Scriptures as they give an account of Job and the Lord's dealing with him.

> Thus the Lord blessed the latter days of Job more than his earlier ones. For he had fourteen thousand sheep, six thousand camels, a thousand yoke of oxen, and a thousand she asses. And he had seven sons and three daughters. . . . In all the land no other women were as beautiful as the daughters of Job; and their father gave them an inheritance among their brethren. After this, Job lived a hundred and forty years; and he saw his children, his grandchildren, and even his great grandchildren. Then Job died, old and full of years.[3]

This points to an unconscious realization that long life is a blessing and is needed for the fulfillment of the personalilty and that long life, or the unique gifts of those who have lived long, are also needed by the society and the culture.

Yet despite this inner wisdom of the gifts of aging, we have developed a youth culture and have consciously demeaned the second half of life. Many adults at the mid-point of their lives have a conscious attitude of being completed with its corresponding haughtiness and pride, and others have a conscious sister attitude of being "washed up." This second form of being completed entails feelings of uselessness, aimlessness, worthlessness, depression, and despair. Whether it be a sense of completion that is over-evaluation, or one of under-evaluation, both are a death blow to the growth of personality that the second half of life calls for.

The second half of life is the call to wholeness, an invitation to continual becoming. It demands a relativization of all the hard acquired strengths, values, goals, ideals, and personality structures of my childhood and youth. Key to this process is the ability to play.

II. Insights on Playing from Carl G. Jung

In *Memories, Dreams, Reflections,* Carl Gustav Jung describes his own mid-life crisis/transition, that movement distinguishing the first half of life from the second. "After the parting of the ways with Freud, a period of inner uncertainty began for me."[4] This period of disorientation broke into his life catapulted by the shock of his rupture with Freud and, as a result, with the whole psychoanalytical school of his day. Discredited by his peers, his inner self bore the fruits of this eruption. The young doctor with so much promise, prestige, success and steadfastness entered a period of "inner uncertainty." His ego was being prepared to make a shift. It would diminish in importance and move in value as the unconcious would slowly come to be valued anew and be allowed to emerge so that the Self could become the greater reality. Jung was being called to enter into his mid-life conversion even as St. Paul on the road to Damascus was called. From that experience, both men became nurturers of the Self in others. "Out of his infinite glory, may he give you the power through his Spirit for your hidden self to grow strong. . . ."[5]

When one is "knocked to the ground" by the shock of an illumination, when the outer structure of one's ego is found to be at odds with one's growing awareness and expanding consciousness, one is forced into a period of "disorientation." Jung found it necessary to adapt, at this time, in his practice a lightheartedness toward his patients. This playful attitude compensated for the loss of faith in himself and in his practice. The surety he had had about his style and his procedures and techniques gave way to an attitude that was more laid back and playful. This "new attitude toward his patients" gave birth not only to his own form of analysis and therapy but to his personal style of dream analysis.[6] He did not give up his practice during this time of disorientation but he did change his attitude toward his patients, his system of theory, and style of practice. He also cut down on his work by withdrawing from a teaching engagement in the university. A playful atitude toward his own disequilibrium allowed him in this dark night to hold on in stark faith to his own charism as a doctor even while he suspected there was some psychic disturbance in himself. Speaking of himself during this time Jung says, "I lived as if under constant pressure. At times this became so strong that I suspected there was some psychic disturbance in myself."[7] Listening to his inner self Jung responded to his inner inclination to literally return to a childhood occupation of playing passionately with building blocks and sand. That period of childhood, he recalled, was filled with enthusiastic creativity and he longed to contact the creative life of that boy long ago. At first it was a blow to his pride, to his ego, to find himself building "cottages," "castles" and "villages." But soon the spirit of play took over and with great enthusiasm he found himself taken up with the creative activity of play. Here he forgot himself, was lifted out of his disorientation, and his imagination was set free. "In the course of this activity my thoughts clarified, and I was able to grasp the fantasies whose presence in myself I dimly felt."[8] The creative child was released in Jung and he was on his way to discovering his own personal myth and story that gave way to his second journey, the second half of his life.

This experience of playing in sand became a pattern in his life. Often during the second half of his life he turned to using his hands in a creative way to relieve stress, to foster the flow of thought and fantasy, to illuminate his spirit in times of darkness, to keep the child alive in himself. Following the death of his wife, Emma, Jung turned to sculpturing in stone. This grieving in stone helped him to suffer his loss and come to acceptance and peace.

Jung's play with sand marked the beginning of his mid-life crisis/transition and his play with mandalas marked the end of this long decade of travail. He was being forced, compelled during these years to attend to his inner world. The forces of his unconscious came to him in play, fantasy, emotions, and negative feelings. As his inner world became more and more real, there grew a greater discrepancy between his inner and outer life. He knew he had to maintain both, as he suspected both were integral to who he really was. His family life and his professional work became the rocks and foundation to which he joyfully rooted himself as his islands of reality while he explored his own unconscious psyche. He had come to sense that the unconscious was the source of all creativity and of the flowering of the personality in the second half of life.

Jung's mandala drawings at this time were primarily sketched in a little black book. Each morning for a period of time he sketched "a small circular drawing" which seemed to correspond to his inner situation and allowed him to observe his psychic transformations taking place day by day. The need to use his hands, to use play as a means to express and objectify the movements within himself, were witness to the individuation taking place in him. Psychic objectivity became more real with the expression of each mandala drawing, and the integration of the conscious and unconscious was portrayed in them. Jung was coming to a new and a transformed equilibrium. He was becoming centered. The ego which had lost its hold and grip upon the personality back at the start of this phase had shifted. The Self was centered and central. The unconscious would continue to be at the service of the Self, as would the ego allowing development of personality to go on all through the second half of his life.

In Jung's personal life the attitude of playfulness and play itself was an important ingredient, if not the medium itself, that fostered the process of individuation within him. This was so not only during those years of disorientation following his break with Freud, but it continued into his later life right up until his death on June 6, 1961. Listen to him describe his life in those years.

> At times I feel as if I am spread out over the landscape and inside things, and am myself living in every tree, in the splashing of the waves, in the clouds and the animals that come and go, in the procession of the seasons. . . . I live in modest harmony with nature. Thoughts rise to the surface which reach back into the centuries, and accordingly anticipate a remote future. Here the torment of creation is lessened; creativity and play are close together.[9]

What playfulness we observe in him when he is entertained for over an hour fascinated by a concert coming from the fireplace where he is boiling water for an evening bath!

> The water began to boil and the kettle to sing. It sounded like many voices, or stringed instruments, or even like a whole orchestra. . . . I sat and listened, fascinated. For far

> more than an hour I listened to the concert, to this natural melody. It was soft music, containing, as well, all the discord of nature. And that was right, for nature is not only harmonious; she is also dreadfully contradictory and chaotic. The music was that way too. . . .[10]

This experience shows us someone willing to surrender to the playful experience of the moment. Play is bound up with the mystery of life and breaks in upon us even as mystery does. The flirting of play is an invitation to let go of our preoccupations and goal centeredness and become, for a time, a child again. Play is a legitimate preoccupation for the adult as well as the child. Play allows us to be free, to be lighthearted, to relish in enjoyment, and to bring together in a glorious symphony all kinds of sounds. Nature is harmonious and yet both contradictory and chaotic. This is part of the experience of becoming individuated. Opposing factors, being held onto despite their contradictions, come together in a glorious symphony. Our onesidedness gives way to our holding onto opposing and contradictory positions: good/bad, masculine/feminine, life/death, feeling/thinking, sensing/intuiting, rational/irrational, inner life/outer life, consciousness/unconsciousness, personal/transpersonal, growth/decay, conflict/harmony, dependence/independence, joy/suffering. Holding onto these polarities and contradictions is painful. Things appear not right. Certitude is gone and with it one's goals, values and direction. But a symphony of wholeness emerges out of this chaos and the irreconcilable becomes as one. The coming together of chaos is a creative thing. The creation narratives in the Book of Genesis depict God the Creator bringing order out of chaos. In the writings of the prophet Jeremiah we see the Lord, the potter, creating a new being out of a marred and deformed vessel. This can help to convince us that creation out of chaos is the norm, not the exception.

Wholeness and integration do not come to the one who holds off consciousness, who refuses to respond to growing awareness. To deny the good in opposing values, to repress or suppress messages of one's unconscious personality, is to deny the creative power within the chaos and therefore to deny the new order or new being one is destined to be. Mandala drawings or visions are not only the sign of accomplished integration but the source of coming integration and the symbolic sign pointing the way toward the longed-for wholeness or individuation. The wholeness and the new order are all within us. It is only a case of incarnating it in our own image of Self, and in our outward expression or imaging of that Self. "The mandala serves a conservative purpose—namely, to restore a previously existing order. But it also serves the creative purpose of giving expression and form to something that does not yet exist, something new and unique."[11]

Play allows us to listen to the inner Self. It allows us to image other ways of being. It opens up avenues to our unconscious, creating an atmosphere and an environment for the becoming of the Self. Jung tells us that when the ability to listen inward is great, there is a corresponding need to listen to another voice, the voice of nature.[12] Nature has for each of us a deep down inner strength and wisdom to communicate to us. In communication with nature our inner Self is called forth and made vulnerable. The ego surrenders under this numinous experience and one is more open to see things as they really are. Nature creates for us an enclosed island where we can be, where we can become. More and more in the second half of life we each need our little islands. When Jung was asked if he had an "island of peace" which offered him a "refuge in the streams of daily living," he replied, "It is not so easy to answer your question about the 'island of peace.' I seem to have quite an archipelago. Some of the main islands are: my garden, the view of distant mountains, my country place where I withdraw from the noise of the city life, my library. Also small things like books, pictures, stones."[13] We all need an archipelago that is truly our own, little islands where we can let go and play. Here in play the unconscious the unfolding of the Self takes place. We need our islands to play and to pray. Both playing and praying keep us in contact with the unconscious dimension of ourselves. The inner center is realized in playing and praying.

Our islands need not always be solitary ones. In Jung's later days he had a small group of friends with whom he went on small auto excursions to the countryside. They playfully called it the ITCRA (International Touring And Culinary Research Association). This seems to be a real pun on adult life as we know it. To be acceptable our adult activities have to be about serious things like "research." "Humor mocks the serious business of the world and the mighty who carry it out."[14] While on our archipelago we come to experience our latent wholeness and move it toward greater realization. Jung tells us that "the experience of wholeness is . . . an extremely simple matter of feeling yourself in harmony with the whole world within and without."[15]

III. Praying and Playing

For each of us our island experience be it playing or praying, is an invitation to "cease striving and know that I am God."[16] Often individuation and growth are presented as a lot of hard work. Yet it appears that the image of nature, letting go, one season following another, the falling of a seed into the ground, the opening of a rose—all depict a gentle movement and acceptance of the natural order. We are waiting in this time of growth and individuation for the secret to our being. What we "are waiting for will come, if it comes at all, silently, 'on dove's feet' into the individual's heart. It will be something that is continously born in beauty like a fountain in sunlight, out of endless rhythmic interplay of opposites."[17]

Both playing and praying are an invitation to experience the "way things really are." Here we need no pretenses. We can put our terrible responsibility into the hands of the Other. Playing and praying are often the source for us of genuine mystical experience. Speaking of this Andrew Greeley says,

> The mystical experience seems to be reasonably common. It involves a breaking from daily experiences of time and play and a search for some sort of basic primitive union with the Way Things Really Are. While in its origins it was certainly religious, it need not be religious for people today, in the sense that it need not have a special theological or denominational context. However, in its attempt to come to grips experientially with the Way Things Really Are, the mystical is implicity and fundamentally religious. . . . It is usually triggered by some sort of experience of goodness, truth, beauty or pleasure that apparently predisposes the person for the mystical event by taking the mind off ordinary events and making him temporarily passive so that "reality may rush in.". . . Peace, joy, union, insight, love, confidence seem to take possession of the

> person. . . . Finally, the "ecstatic comes down" from his moments of rapture with new serenity and confidence for his daily life.[18]

Such mystical moments are realizations of "The Kingdom of God is within you."[19] They prefigure a time of greater integration, the period of increased individuation as well as the day when we fully experience "what eye hath not seen nor ear heard."

If we are to be truly committed to our own growth in the second half of life we must be intent on making prayer and play a greater and greater reality in our life. One must first come to see and experience personal and spiritual growth as the religious response to the gift of life. To continue to grow and become is to be engaged in the truest worship. Worship is the creature's response in awe, gratitude and wonder at the work of the Creator. To take the life he has given us and foster its growth and development is to respond authentically in awe, gratitude, and wonder at the Creator's creation. Once we have nurtured our own growth and our commitment to growth in ourself we have the equipment for nurturing the personal and spiritual growth of others. Praying and playing allow us to relativize our own growth and our commitment to it. Praying and playing open for us possibilities for growth that we never would have dreamed of. Praying and playing allow us to trust and believe in the outcome of our existence even while we are on the way. Prayer and play allow us to imagine other ways of being, other orders and patterns of self and society. Prayer and play allow us to distance ourselves from the centrality of our causes, our work, our ministry, our preoccupations. Prayer and play open us to the other side of everything and cure us of our terrible onesidedness. Prayer and play allow us to image other sides of self, our shadow, our contra-sexuality, our inferior functions, and archetypal patterns dormant within us. Prayer and play connect us to our deepest Self. Prayer and play let us realize how much more there is to us than our ego. Prayer and play let us experience the Creator in new and unfathomable ways. Prayer and play connect us to the deep inner recesses of our personality. Prayer and play unite us to the world of people outside ourself, to the glories of nature and to the accomplishments of other generations and our own contemporaries. Prayer and play make my living and working more Godlike.

In play, it is evident that I am made in the image and likeness of God who gently gives us a lifetime to grow and become and gives time to this universe of ours to grow into full consciousness. Peter Berger's words come to mind here, "To find courage to do what must be done in a given moment is not the only moral good. It is also very much a moral good that this same moment does not become the be-all and end-all of one's existence, that in meeting its demands one does not lose the capacity to laugh and to play."[20] The mid-point of our lives is the time to rediscover and develop our capacity to play. With this renewed capacity the flowering of our personality will come about.

Listen to Jung, our world-renowned author, doctor, psychiatrist, analyst, theorist, teacher, as he describes how he spends his time in his latter days.

> Here too the weather has been indescribably beautiful, and this has most effectively prevented me from writing letters, but instead I have finished painting the ceiling in Bollingen and done more work on my inscription and—last but not least—rebricked the rivulets to prevent seepage and cooked some good meals and found and bought an excellent wine. All this has rested me and cured me of various vexations.[21]

The rediscovery of the art of play is indispensable to the individuation that takes place in the second half of life. With Jung it was crucial in the breakthrough from the first half of life to the second, from the development of the ego to the development of the Self. It was also crucial for the ongoing personality development in his old age. The ability to enjoy, to experience pleasure is a human capacity to delight in this world of ours. Play opens us to that enjoyment. "Pleasuring is like a muscle that needs to be exercised or it becomes weakened or useless."[22] "I believe that more people die from lack of fulfillment and pleasure than from any other cause."[23] There may be a connection with our willingness to enter into enjoyment and pleasure in this time and place and our capacity for enjoyment and pleasure in eternal life. How can you love and enjoy God in the next world if you cannot love and enjoy God in this world?

The need for play comes from an inner demand of our psyche, not from an outer prescription or law for successfully living the second half of life. We begin in various ways to experience the need to execute the other side of our personality. Other things begin to call us from within and without. Tunes we never heard before begin to resonate in our being. It is a call to the fullness of life: "Unless a man is born again of water and the spirit. . . ."[24] Unless the coming together of all the fragments of our person takes place, you shall not enter the Kingdom of heaven, the place God has prepared for you from all eternity, your own wholeness and unity with all of creation and the Creator. Play allows that integration and wholeness to take place.

Leo Lionni, an author of children's books, tells a captivating story about a field mouse, Frederick.[25] It is a story that sings a hymn of praise to the gentle art of playing and praying. Frederick sees the more in the daily occupations and goals of the field mice. He knows the need of wasting time in play and enjoyment. Frederick drank in the rays of the sun as the other mice worked hard at gathering food for the long cold winter.

> Do not store up for yourselves treasures on earth, where moths and woodworms destroy them and thieves can break in and steal. For where your treasure is there will your heart be also.[26]

Frederick also spent his time drinking in the beautiful colors all around him, and in fantasy and dreaming he finds words to express the mysteries that he is experiencing. Frederick knows that his experience of the sun will help them all transcend the long cold winter. He knows that the memory of pleasuring in bright colors will help dispel the cold dark gray of winter.

> I tell you most solemnly, it was not Moses who gave you bread from heaven. It is my Father who gives you the bread from heaven, the true bread; for the bread of God is that which comes down from heaven and gives life to the world.[27]

And Frederick knows also that the ability to dream and put his dreams in words will help them all visualize the spring that is too long in coming and will give meaning to the experience they are having. Dreams will contact the myths and symbols that will express the deep-down meaning of their lives.

> Whoever drinks this water will get thirsty again, but anyone who drinks the water that I shall give will never be thirsty again; the water that I shall give will turn into a spring inside him, welling up to eternal life.[28]

Winter came with its snow and ice and the little field mice were locked into their underground winter home stocked with food which the field mice had gathered while Frederick was busy in enjoyment and fantasy. In the beginning of winter, life was happy, but too soon the cupboard was bare, the mice were cold and hungry and their spirits were down. But then they remembered Frederick! They called on him to use his supply of sunrays, colors and words. Even as Frederick recalled his experience of the sun, the field mice were warmed by the memory. It became as a living experience for each of them. When Frederick described the colors, each mouse could see them as vividly as Frederick had weeks before. This ability to imagine excited them so that they forgot their cold and hunger; indeed they were filled with color. Then Frederick recalled his fantasies and his words fell upon each of them explaining the meaning of their lives and filling them with joyful acceptance, hope and expectations.

> Who scatters snowflakes? Who melts the ice? Who spoils the weather? Who makes it nice? Who grows the four leaf clovers in June? Who dims the daylight? Who lights the moon? Four little field mice who live in the sky. Four little field mice . . . like you and I.[29]

Frederick goes on to say that the Springmouse turns on showers, the Summermouse paints the flowers, the Fallmouse gives walnuts and wheat and the Wintermouse comes with little cold feet. This is truly a tale for each person called to live fully the second half of life. The busy ego activity of the first half of life must be given up for the splendor of "deep down things." This is the time for questions: Is this all there is? What is my life all about? What is the meaning of all this? Who am I? Where are we going? Is there a God?

By giving way to play we open ourself to the transcendent dimension of life. Like Frederick we come to know what really matters, the manna that will never run out, the well that has living waters. Frederick came to have a larger view of Self and did not keep it to himself but became himself living water and living manna for others. Frederick paid heed to the invitations from within, "Don't work too much."

Notes

1. C.G. Jung, *Letters*, ed. Gerhard Adler and Aniela Jaffe, trans. R.F.C. Hull, Vol. 2: 1951–1961 (Princeton: Princeton University Press, 1953–), p. 25.
2. Anne Morrow Lindberg, *Gift from the Sea* (New York: Vintage Books Edition, 1978), pp. 16–17.
3. Job 42:12–13, 15–17.
4. C.G. Jung, *Memories, Dreams, Reflections*, ed. Aniela Jaffe, trans. Richard and Clara Winston (New York: Vintage Books, 1965), p. 170.
5. Eph 3:16.
6. C.G. Jung, *Memories, Dreams, Reflections*, p. 171.
7. *Ibid.*, p. 173.
8. *Ibid.*, p. 174.
9. *Ibid.*, pp. 225–226.
10. *Ibid.*, p. 229.
11. M.-L. von Franz, "The Process of Individuation," *Man and His Symbols*, ed. Carl G. Jung (New York: Doubleday and Co., 1964), p. 225.
12. C.G. Jung, *Letters*, Vol. 2: 1951–1961, p. 21.
13. *Ibid.*, p. 40.
14. Peter Berger, *A Rumor of Angels*, p. 88.
15. C.G. Jung, *Letters*, p. 456.
16. Ps 46:11.
17. Alan McGlashan, *Gravity and Levity* (Boston: Houghton Mifflin Company, 1976), p. 136.
18. Andrew Greeley, *Ecstasy: A Way of Knowing*, (New Jersey: Prentice-Hall Inc., 1974), p. 48.
19. Lk 17:21.
20. C.G. Jung, *Letters*, p. 351.

22. Lillian R. Dangott and Richard A. Kalish, *A Time To Grow* (New Jersey: Prentice-Hall Inc., 1979), p. 162.

23. *Ibid.*, p. 163.

24. Jn 3:5.

25. Leo Lionni, *Frederick* (New York: Random House Pantheon Books, 1967).

26. Mt 6:19–21.

27. Jn 6:32–33.

28. Jn 4:14.

29. Leo Lionni, *Frederick*, p. 84.

CHAPTER 8

Play and Personal Spirituality

I. The Dream

I woke up from my dream in the middle of the night. This had never happened to me before and it has never happened since. Immediately I got out of bed and went into the kitchen to recall and write down what I had experienced. I felt compelled as Joseph did when he heard in a dream the command: "Get up, take the child and his mother, and flee to Egypt. Stay there until I tell you otherwise. Herod is searching for the child to destroy him" (Mt 2:13). From the very start my dream had an emotional overtone that involved my total being. It still has that impact upon me as I write about it now, recall it privately or talk about it with others. My dream is like a treasure given to me as pure graciousness. When I recall last year and all the events that occurred, that dream is listed first, of prime importance. It is like a living part of me, not just something I dreamed ten months ago but a dream that revealed what had been going on in me, what was going on in me and what was to continue going on in me in the days, months and years ahead. This is the dream.

We had just finished a mid-life workshop. As usual we came out completely drained. We had poured ourselves out in the giving and now we got into the car for the long drive home. Another sister was with us. I was driving. We were tired and hungry. We wanted to stop for something to eat. I was anything but composed. I could feel the tension all over my body. I started to drive into the darkness. The road and the vicinity were unfamiliar to me. It started to rain heavily, making the night driving even more difficult. My body was arched as I peered through the windshield into the night. Suddenly the headlights of an oncoming car glared into our front window. Quickly I directed the car over to the right. Either not knowing or forgetting I was on a two way street, I had been on the left side of the road toward the oncoming traffic. Now I was angry. I complained, "I don't know where I am going."

Suddenly the night began to lift. I recognized where we were and the road ahead of us. With a little relief, but still tense and upset, I said, "It's all right. Now I know where we are." But then, before I knew what had happened, our car was climbing a hill. I cried out, "Oh, no. We are going right back where we came from. We are doing it all over again." It appeared to me that this road was taking us right back to where we had come from.

At this moment daylight broke around us and some beautiful birds, perhaps seagulls, flew overhead. It was then that the physical and emotional upset left me. I forgot about trying to get us home and have some supper. The responsibility of driving, the exhaustion and hunger that had been mine, all that dissolved. We spotted a sign that read: "Meditation this morning." We passed a man and we called out to him, "Where is the meditation going to be?" "On top of the hill," he called back to us. "Just drive up to the top of the hill and you will find it in the heart-shaped building." Then we noticed, in the now full sunlight, that there was a single file procession of people, many with backpacks climbing up a narrow path on the mountainside.

Everything in me was changed. The anxiety, tension, anger, upset had totally lifted. It was as though the morning sun was in me. The early play of the birds had dispelled all my seriousness, discontent, ill humor. I forgot about everything and was lifted into the joy of that quiet, beautiful, expectant moment. As we reached the top of the hill, we saw standing before us a large beautifully shining front marble entrance, shaped like a heart. People, all relaxed and tension free, were entering through the marble entrance. I made note of the fact that this marble heart was identical to the marble heart in the sanctuary, high up, over the altar in our parish church. When we went through the entrance we found a beautiful outdoor church. It was a meditation garden. People were praying and playing. Some sat on the grass and under trees. There was music. There was a mixture of quiet serenity, peacefulness, and intense joy and ecstasy. Then I woke up.

Immediately I knew the message from my unconscious. The spirit deep within me was giving the warning, "We are going right back where we came from. We are doing it all over again." I knew intuitively what the meaning was. I knew the rightness of the judgment and the seriousness of the warning. It was that I am being called to surrender my striving so terribly hard, with such fanatical onesidedness for the goals before me. That striving is part and parcel of the beauty of youth. It was the fruit of the spirit within and without me. But now the spirit is present in my deep inner need to let go, to realize that the kingdom of God is within me, within the culture, within the universe. The movement of the Spirit is within the joys and sorrows, the gladness and pain, the wholeness and the fracturedness of each and all of us. As I rejoice in the intense activity and restlessness of the young adults around me I must embrace the other spectrum as well, transforming my style of working and living. The mystery is that what we all work so hard for does in fact exist already. We are all in process and my major contribution to this divine process is to know now the endtime and to live in the knowledge. Even as I continue to work for justice and peace and wholeness, and pray, "Your kingdom come, your will be done" (Mt 6:10), I am being called to experience in joy the reality of that Kingdom.

> Joy is play's intention. When this intention is actually realized, in joyful play, the time structure of the playful universe takes on a very specific quality—namely, it becomes eternity.[1]

Very practically, I am being called to let praying and playing become the primary factors for personality development within me. I am being called not to go about my ministry and my living with the same intensity, single-mindedness and onesidedness that was so appropriate in my twenties and thirties. I am being called to let the spirit be the gardener in the depths of my own psyche. I am being called to rejoice in the creation all around me that I have been so busy trying to improve. I am being called to rejoice more in the Spirit's movement rather than simply directing his activity in my forceful struggle for reform. I am being called to enjoy all that is, has been and will be. I am being called to a spirituality of play. This call to play is a call to allow my psychic energy to be withdrawn from my conscious effort to "fill up what is lacking in the suffering of Christ" (Col 1:24), and to allow those energies to be redirected in the arena of playing and praying. This will allow the spirit to make up what is wanting in my own person, the part of creation for which I have the gravest responsibility. The words of Jesus, at this time in my life, are ringing in my ears, "Martha, Martha, you are anxious and upset about many things; one thing only is required" (Lk 10:41).

II. The Child

"Now when Jesus had crossed back to the other side again in the boat, a large crowd gathered around him and he stayed close to the lake. One of the officials of the synagogue, a man named Jairus, came near. Seeing Jesus, he fell at his feet and made this earnest appeal: 'My little daughter is critically ill. Please come and lay your hands on her so that she may get well and live.' The two went off together and a large crowd followed, pushing against Jesus. . . . He had not finished speaking when people from the official's house arrived saying, 'Your daughter is dead. Why bother the Teacher further?' Jesus disregarded the report that had been brought and said to the official: 'Fear is useless. What is needed is trust.' He would not permit anyone to follow him except Peter, James and James' brother John. As they approached the house of the synagogue leader, Jesus was struck by the noise of the people wailing and crying loudly on all sides. He entered and said to them: 'Why do you make this din with your wailing? The child is not dead. She is asleep.' At this they began to ridicule him and he put them all out.

"Jesus took the child's father and mother and his own companions and he entered the room where the child lay. Taking her hand he said to her, 'Talitha, Koum,' which means, 'Little girl, get up.' The girl, a child of twelve, stood up immediately and began to walk around. At this the family's astonishment knew no bounds. He enjoined them strictly not to let anyone know about it, and told them to give her something to eat" (Mk 5:21–24, 35–43).

It is the child in me who is being awakened by this dream, this call. I lost her long ago in all the ego striving of the first half of life. Now the Jairus of that ego turns to the miracle worker and cries out, "My little daughter is critically ill. Please come and lay your hands on her so that she may get well and live" (Mk 5:23).

The Lord loves the Jairus in me. In truth, he helped in his development. The Gospel tells us that Jairus was an official of the synagogue. He represents the well-defined ego, including the persona, so important to our self-image and our relationship to other people and the outer world. It was unorthodox for such a person as Jairus to have recourse to the novel, Jesus of Nazareth. The child that Jairus is concerned about represents part of the unconscious of Jairus and of my unconscious. Jesus is anxious to come to Jairus' assistance. He will free and liberate his inner child. Even as Jairus approaches Jesus with his request we have a glimpse of the self. This movement in Jairus is a reflection of the self, the mediation of the unconscious child and the ego. Throughout the Gospel there is an ongoing relationship between Jairus and the dying daughter as well as the restored child. Jesus shows respect, concern and love for both Jairus (the conscious) and the child (unconscious). The process of individuation calls us to the same respect and love.

> If you ruin your conscious personality, the so-called ego-personality, you deprive the self of its real goal, namely to become real itself. The goal of life is the realization of the self.[2]

"Your daughter is dead," all is hopeless, conversion is impossible, change cannot occur, you are locked into your ego, is what we hear. "Fear is useless. What is needed is trust. . . . The child is not dead. She is asleep." Carl Jung tells us that "the child paves the way for a future change of personality."[3] He goes on to say:

> In the individuation process, it anticipates the figure that comes from the synthesis of conscious and unconscious elements in the personality. It is therefore a symbol which unites the opposites, a mediator, bringer of healing, that is, one who makes whole.[4]

The crowds laugh within us as they laugh in the Gospel. But the Lord puts them all out, makes them leave. Taking the child by her hand the Lord says to her, "Talitha, koum. . . . Little girl, get up." This was the call in my mid-life dream, as well as the call to nurture that child's life in us, "give her something to eat." Jesus commands the mother and the father of the little girl to keep her alive. Each of us is commanded to nourish the child within us. This child will renew one's spirit. She will restore one's equilibrium. She will be the source of creativity and zest for life in us.

We all know that an essential food of every child is play. Peter Berger tells us that "in later life play brings about a beatific reiteration of childhood."[5] We are being called to a whole new way of existence in the second half of life. The child in us and playing and playfulness are the keys to that new being, to that new existence.

When we allow ourselves to work hard setting goals and moving toward achieving them we are "filling up what is lacking in the sufferings of Christ," but when we allow the child within to come alive we are allowing the Lord to provide for us in these simple esctatic interludes, simply recognizing what is—the presence of graciousness in all that is. The child delights in the moment. The adult sees the problems, faults, incompleteness, and refuses to, cannot relish the moment. Yet now, in the second half of life, the adult is called to let the child live, to let it relish the pure delight of the moment. All future growth is dependent on the life of this inner child.

> The developing adult is assumed to incorporate positively the individual and (in fact) irrepressible character of the child. Adulthood assumes that the child cannot be left behind, but is the basis of the mature personality.[6]

The awakening of the child in the second half of life signifies the awakening of a new attitude toward life. "As we have to learn again and again, that faith in God's presence and not will power is the basis of salvation and holiness."[7] This "new attitude" is found within our inner child. It is a call to conversion. This process of conversion calls for continual nourishment of the child in play. We are being called, in mid-life, to a spirituality of play. A person's spirituality is his or her personal pattern of life that flows from his or her own particular theology and attitude. A spirituality of play flows from one's basic orientation toward life as mediating the gracious presence of a loving other. It incorporates a playful (including prayerful) attitude toward life itself as well as a life style that has a rhythm of time given to playing (including praying). Harvey Cox tells us that human play is our capacity for festivity and fantasy. A spirituality of play feeds upon the human capacity for festivity and fantasy inherent in the child. Playing and praying puts us in contact with the unconscious dimension of ourself. The inner center is realized in praying and playing. In some way we can make real the Messianic vision: "Old men and old women will again sit down in the square of Jerusalem. The city shall be filled with boys and girls playing in the streets. . . . But now I will not deal with the remnant of this people as in former days, says the Lord of hosts, for it is the seedtime of peace; the vine shall yield its fruit, the land shall bear its crops, and the heavens shall give their dew. All these things I will have the remnant of the people possess" (Zech 8:4–5, 11–12). "Go up to the top of the hill and enter the heart shaped building."

III. The Conversion

In each season of my life cycle I am called to a new dimension of becoming in the related areas of physical, emotional, psychological, relational and spiritual growth. My image of myself changes as I experience a movement within my own person and my consciousness of self and the world expands. In playing and praying I come to experience myself as much more than all my ego defines me as.

> To play is to yield oneself to a kind of magic, to enact to oneself the absolutely other, to pre-empt the future, to give the lie to the inconvenient world of fact. In play earthly realities become, of a sudden, things of transient moment, presently left behind, then disposed of and buried in the past; the mind is prepared to accept the unimagined and incredible, to enter a world where different laws apply, to be relieved of all the weights that bear it down, to be free, kingly, unfettered, divine.[8]

Commenting on these words, Cox tells us that Rahner "describes play in words that could be used almost verbatim to describe pray."[9] When I play, all the things that so concern me are relativized and whole other parts of my person are freed. Play releases me from the bondage of consciousness and allows the rivers of the unconscious to be undammed. To allow oneself to play and to pray is to place upon your unconscious personality the respect and awe that it is calling for. It has long been the tradition of the Church to invite us to pay attention to the "divine indwelling." We were being reminded to look for the divine within as well as without.

> To cleave to God hidden beneath the inward and outward forces which animate our being and sustain it in its development is ultimately to open ourselves to, and put trust in, all the breaths of life.[10]

Our inner world is the locus of the divine, as well as the creation outside of us.

> Before Christ's coming, men may have sought the invisible God in temples and shrines; after his coming, they seek him in human life. What is revealed in Christ is that human life is the locus of the divine.[11]

Like Symeon the tenth century theologian we are now to seek God in the world in vain, as we are being asked to allow God to rise, like a little sun, in our own heart.[12]

A spirituality of play is to act out of my belief that the locus of the divine is my own humanity as well as all humanity. In the second half of life the inner depths of our humanity, our own unconscious personality are the seeds of new growth and the wellsprings of the Spirit. That is what the dream was telling me. "Go up to the top of the hill and there you will find a heart shaped building. Enter the heart shaped building for the morning meditation." Our spiritual tradition has always seen the inner world of a person as a cathedral. Jesus told us: "The reign of God is already in your midst" (Lk 17:21). When I entered the heart shaped building, similar to the vision of Zechariah, I found people playing and praying. Both prayer and play are calling us to the unconscious dimension of self. In the second half of life we are each called to a new dimension of growth as radically different as was the growth that occurred in the adolescent transition. This new level of growth calls for a new and transformed attitude and the means of the transformation process continuing. In the beginning we must make an act of will to play.

> Man must decide to play. He has to turn aside from an immediate field of tension and from the workaday world so as to enter fully into the new world of play.[13]

As we begin to experience the fruit of this play and to see ourselves in a new way, both playing and praying will become as important to us as the work, service, ministry and relationships that have defined us, mediated the good to us and been the avenues that allowed us to express the spirit within us. Carl Jung tells us that the flowering of the personality is rooted in the unconscious. Playing and praying are like a "halfway house" between our inner and outer world. Whether we enter the playground or the cathedral within us, the imagery found there puts us in contact with our own latent resources and powers. Our conscious ego serves us well here as it is our ego strength that is needed to make concrete in our real life situation of living, working, playing, praying outer forms and structures to embody the awakened imagery within. As we repattern our style of living and find new direction for our second journey, the relationship of our inner and outer world is seen as crucial in the way we give ourselves to both playing and praying. Both become more and more crucial to the quality of our life.

At this point in life, play is as important a force for forging a new path and for development of personality as play was in infancy and early childhood. A child plays at being a hero, being "grownup," being a monster, being a mother, being a father, etc. Each aspect of the child's play is the spiritual force for growth. In the second half of life I am called to know experientially that the conscious self is not the consummation of life. I am called to continue the voyage of discovery.

> To hear the soul's speech, psyche's logos in words, one must relax the limbs as if in love, as if asleep, as if in death. In such states, one cannot do anything. Limb-relaxing leads to inaction of body, a paralysis of will and a lowering of ego consciousness. This state is the essential condition to see and hear the cares and concerns of soul.[14]

I know my dream to represent not only my personal call to a new mode of being but the universal call to all people on the second journey. The second journey is not like the first. I was well warned, "You are doing it all over again, going right back from where you came." Letting go of my concern and consciousness, surrendering to the new dawn I entered the heart shaped building, and the experience of the archetypal Self emerged in the centering of all my deepest longings for unity expressed in the cathedral within. This is the universal call to conversion—to allow the child to be born in you, to be born again of "water and the spirit," to surrender to the unconscious in prayer and play. This ongoing conversion is living out of a spirituality of play.

I know I am not a child and never can be one again. I am not equal to any one other aspect of my unconscious. I am not Jairus. I am not the Jairus of my ego or my unconscious (masculine, feminine, father, mother, savior, hero, reformer, warrior). Still each of these is a genuine part of me; when they can be together, interact and relate, co-exist, the Self is becoming a greater reality. Each is a shining glimmer of the divine reality, but only in the wholeness is the Self fully realized. This is the spirituality of play: playing with the opposites, playing with the conscious and the unconscious. To play with the unconscious I must believe in it, take it seriously. The process of growth, individuation calls for this attitude toward the unconscious. The archetypal Self in my dream and the universal call that it represents is similarly demonstrated in a dream recorded by Carl Jung in *Memories, Dreams and Reflections.* John Welch gives an account of this same dream in his book, *Spiritual Pilgrims: Carl Jung and Teresa of Avila.*

> I found myself in a dirty, sooty city. It was night, and winter, and dark, and raining. I was in Liverpool. With a number of Swiss—say, half a dozen—I walked through the dark streets. I had the feeling that there we were coming from the harbor, and that the real city was actually up above, on the cliffs. We climbed up there. It reminded me of Basel, where the market is down below and then you go up through the Totengasschen (Alley of the Dead), which leads to a plateau above and so to the Petersplatz and the Peterskirche. When we reached the plateau, we found a broad square dimly illuminated by street lights, into which many streets converged. The various quarters of the city were arranged radically around the square. In the center was a round pool, and in the middle of it a small island. While everything round about was obscured by rain, fog, smoke and dimly lit darkness, the little island blazed with sunlight. On it stood a single tree, a magnolia, in a shower of reddish blossoms. It was as though the tree stood in the sunlight and were at the same time the source of light. My companions commented on the abominable weather, and obviously did not see the tree. They spoke of another Swiss who was living in Liverpool, and expressed surprise that he should have settled here. I was carried away by the beauty of the flowering tree and the sunlit island, and

> thought, "I know very well why he has settled here." Then I awoke.[15]

Speaking of the dream Jung goes on to say:

> This dream represented my situation at the time. . . . Everything was extremely unpleasant, black and opaque—just as I felt then. But I had had a vision of unearthly beauty, and that was why I was able to live at all. Liverpool is the "pool of life. . . . Through this dream I understood that the self is the principle and archetype of orientation and meaning. Therein lies its healing function."[16]

Without this dream Jung tells us he feels he would have lost his orientation. He too felt that his dream was "an act of grace." From it emerged his own personal myth.

My own personal myth is emerging from my dream also, as I continue to relate to it. Play is calling me not only to the life of the spirit as we traditionally think of it but to a reconnection with my own humanity in all its earthly connections. This is so important to avoid a pseudo-centering. Life today can so alienate us from our own physical being and our own need for sensuality. Even Carl Jung, with his continual search for understanding the Self, the process of individuation in all its dimensions, had to take into consideration his whole bodily organism. As an intuitive thinker he needed the balance of sensing and feeling. His later life gives proof to a spirituality of play as part of the art of his living.

Sister Jose Hobday tells the story of Teresa of Avila being questioned by one of her novices about the zest with which she entered into eating one of their rare holiday meals. The novice was quite taken back by such a lack of asceticism on the part of her director of prayer and the spiritual way. Sister Hobday tells us that Teresa laughed when questioned and said: "My dear, when I pray—I pray, and when I eat—I eat." It is a quality of genuine maturity in the second half of life to know the delicate connection between body and spirit. Dietrich Bonhoffer came to know this deep but delicate connection. We find him, while in prison, longing for the natural spirituality of nature as expressed in the seriousness of the sun and his own animality. While in prison he wrote:

> I should like to feel the full force of the sun again, making the skin hot and the whole body glow, and reminding me that I am a corporeal being. I should like to be tired by the sun, instead of by books and thoughts. I should like to have it awaken my animal existence—I should like not just to see the sun and sip at it a little, but to experience it bodily.[17]

IV. Jesus, the Christ

Can I find a spirituality of play in the Gospels? Did Jesus incorporate into his life style both an attitude of play and a rhythm of time out for play? Reading between the lines, and this is the richest way of reading, I see a Jesus willing to play with Zacchaeus, the Samaritan woman and so many others. His attitude of playfulness in their regard gave him his way in with each of them. Because of it he did not have to equate Zacchaeus or the Samaritan woman with their reputation or the reality of their sinfulness. He could even transform the very vice that held them prisoner and use it in their personal transformation and for his own purposes. The Zacchaeus story has always struck us as comical. Perhaps our own moralism kept us from laughing with delight at this humorous encounter. Zacchaeus, "the chief tax collector and a wealthy man," being small of stature drops all his pretenses, his persona and gives in to his desire to see Jesus by climbing a tree! Jesus, delighted with the whole thing, responds to the largeness of this small man. Then comes the comic surprise Jesus gives the people—he does not honor the righteous with his presence but chooses the despised tax collector. Within Zacchaeus' greed Jesus sees a desire for zestful living. Zacchaeus' shrewdness and money-wise aplomb is put to good use. "I give half my belongings, Lord, to the poor. If I have defrauded anyone in the least, I pay him back fourfold" (Lk 19:8).

With the Samaritan woman Jesus uses the very real occasion of drawing water from a well to get to the heart of the matter. Once again he knows that her promiscuity is a cover-up for her own deep longing desire to be known, a desire for her spirit and inner being to be touched. The discourse that follows is filled with playful intimacy and it allows the woman to contact her own depths and longings. "Give me this water, sir, so that I shall not grow thirsty and have to keep coming here to draw water" (Lk 4:15). This woman of the town was well known by all, and Jesus could not have chosen anyone more capable of making the good news heard quickly and convincingly. "Many Samaritans from that town believed in him on the strength of the woman's word of testimony: 'He told me everything I ever did' " (Jn 4:39). It was the playful attitude of Jesus that allowed the Samaritan woman to be won over by Jesus and to be opened up to other dimensions of herself and of him. Sometimes play alone can allow us not to equate ourself or others with the shadow and to find the pearl within it.

I see in the Gospels a Jesus so playfully familiar with nature and the earthly dimension of life that he continually uses them in his teaching. The teachings of Jesus reveal someone familiar and intimate with the common ordinary life around him. Only someone who had himself become ecstatic in the beauty of nature could have talked about the "Lilies of the Field" the way he did. Only someone touched by the mother hen's attitude toward her chicks could have cried over Jerusalem and made the comparison that he made. Jesus must have played, spent time with, observed lovingly and prayerfully the mustard seed, the grain of wheat, the pearl of great price, the sower, the shepherd with his sheep, the maidens with their oil lamps, the vine and the branches and so many others. As Jesus "wasted time" enraptured by these scenes he saw the unique beauty underlying each and connected it to his own deep resources and to the life and experience of each of us.

I see in the Gospels a Jesus who played the "Game of Intimacy." Allowing oneself to be awakened to companioning others in life is responding to the intimacy of friendship. For all of us there is some other or others out there with whom there will be a mutual response, a tending toward each other in a rhythm of mutual love. Haven't we all been touched by that line in John's discourse at the Last Supper: "One of them, the disciple whom Jesus loved, reclined close to him as they ate" (Jn 13:22). It would be good for us to let that line sink in to us with all that it stands for. Friendship and intimacy take time. They are born out of a willingness and delight in being with each other. Jesus took time for this "game of intimacy." Remember a similar line to the one above in the account of the raising of Lazarus? "The sisters sent word to Jesus to inform him, 'Lord, the one you love is sick' " (Jn 11:3), and again, and "Jesus loved Martha and her sister and Lazarus very much" (Jn 11:5). He shared with James and Peter and John his most intimate moments, depth moments of divine presence and agony, the transfiguration and Gethsemane.

Totally involved in the outer world he was no stranger to his own inner depths and dimensions. How else did he come to know, "Whoever has seen me has seen the Father" (Jn 14:9). Nor was he a stranger to the collective unconscious in its negative and positive aspects. "And I—once I am lifted up from earth—will draw all men to myself" (Jn 12:32). "Why do you question me about what is good? There is One who is good" (Mt 19:17). "Not on bread alone shall man live" (Lk 4:4). "You shall not put the Lord your God to the test" (Lk 4:12). "Do not live in fear, little flock. It has pleased your Father to give you the Kingdom. Sell what you have and give alms. Get purses for yourselves that do not wear out, a never-failing treasure with the Lord which no thief comes near nor moth destroys. Wherever your treasure lies, there your heart will be" (Lk 12:32–34).

Jesus had a comfortableness with the sensual and all his senses: touching, hearing, tasting, seeing, smelling. To cure the blind man we find the sensual Jesus spitting on the ground and making a paste with his saliva and the mud. He smears this on the man's eyes. In no way did Jesus shun close contact. The fact is that he sought it out. This contact is at the heart of the man's cure and of his final words in the story, "I do believe, Lord" (Jn 9:38). Many of us lose contact with the most sensuous of all unions, "He who feeds on my flesh and drinks my blood has life eternal, and I will raise him up on the last day. . . . The man who feeds on my flesh and drinks my blood remains in me, and I in him" (Jn 6:54, 56). And when Mary his mother did not fail to insist that he help out the bride and groom at Cana, he fills the jugs with wine that far surpassed the wine first served. Who of us has not been moved by the fact that he lets the fallen woman be so shockingly familiar with him. He allows her to bathe his feet with her tears, dry them with her hair and anoint them with her perfume. John's Gospel tells of another time that Jesus had the same intimate caring. This time it is Mary the sister of Martha who anoints Jesus' feet with costly perfume. Again, Mary wipes his feet with her hair and "the house was filled with the ointment's fragrance" (Jn 12:3). Judas complains about the waste and reminds everyone of the needs of the poor. Who among us has not done the same kind of thing at one time or another? The Lord's words ring in our ear, "The poor you have always with you, but me you will not always have" (Jn 12:8). And this from the same man who said: "Lord, when did we see you hungry or thirsty or away from home or naked or ill or in prison and not attend you in your needs? He will answer them: "I assure you, as often as you neglected to do it to one of these least ones, you neglected to do it to me" (Mt 25:45). Jesus was not ashamed to have something beautiful and costly wasted on him and he did not let that conflict with his radical call to respond to the poor. Jesus knew the need of a child to be fondled. He also knew the need of every adult to keep the child within him or her alive. "Whoever does not accept the reign of God like a little child shall not take part in it" (Mk 10:15), he told the people as he embraced and blessed the little children.

I know a Jesus in the Gospels who played beautifully and respectfully with the law because he knew that it existed for him and for each of us, not we for it. The law is to serve us, not rule us. He cured on the sabbath, socialized with sinners and reached out to the Gentiles. He played the game of life totally, was committed to it, and gave it up regretfully. But in the end he played the game of faith and death, "I assure you: this day you will be with me in paradise" (Lk 23:43). "Father, into your hands I commend my Spirit" (Lk 23:46). He found the joy of presence even in the midst of the agony and dark night of the soul and it wrung a cry of pure faith from him. He so ate and drank that people commented on it. Contrary to the men of his day he befriended women and called them to follow him. Contrary to his day he chose the less traveled road of celibacy. He played the game of wastefulness, not making a God of virtue or of the generosity he called for or of the care for the poor he demanded. He playfully balanced every polarity: young/old, life/death, rich/poor, fast/feast, love/hate, inner/outer, thinking/feeling, sensing/intuition, active/passive, feminine/masculine, compromise/noncompromise, communal/individual, play/work.

To be committed to this Jesus, each of us is called to be committed to his playful attitude toward life and death itself. To follow him I am called to take up my cross. This is not to "cop-out." It is not

> an attempt to discredit modern values (living standards, maturity, structural change, acceptance of the world, intellectual honesty).[18]

This would be a distortion of the cross, doing violence to the spiritual, human journey. The cross is holding onto the polarities, playing with them so that the cross becomes the resurrection.

Carl Jung tells us that "Christ exemplifies the archetype of the Self."[19] "Christ is still the living myth of our culture."[20] Following Christ

> means: getting involved with him and his way and going one's own way—each of us has his own way—in the light of his directions.[21]

Jesus lived a spirituality of play. In everything he had an attitude of play and he freely played. His life from birth till death gives witness to an attitude of playfulness and a rhythm of playing and praying.

> Because of Jesus, encounter with God is possible, not only in success and joy, but also in failure, in melancholy, in sorrow and pain.[22]

Jesus invites each of us to play the game of life fully and he empowers us to do so.

> By following Jesus Christ, (the human person) in the world of today can truly, humanly live, act, suffer and die: in happiness and unhappiness, life and death, sustained by God and helpful to men.[23]

Not only that, but because of Jesus we too can let our child live. It was the child in Jesus that could surrender to the dream of the impossible here on earth and to an eternal life of unity and love. Even as he gave witness to this child-likeness on the cross he gave witness to the most sublime courage of maturity, the courage to die. Our call to play embraces the spirituality of the second half of life: mid-life and the mature years. It is creation-centered and Christ-centered. It is a call to become our own true Self, so much more than I now experience. And all this in a most gentle and playful way—bearing all the contradictions gently. "Where force rules, there is no love, and where love rules, force does not count."[24] It is the child in us and the gift of play that he or she carries that will initiate in each of us in the second half of life an affirmative and positive attitude toward the aging process. The creative, ongoing, dynamic development of the personality that goes on in the last two seasons of our life: mid-life and the mature years is the fruit of the child, the youth and the adult living within us. Our own personal spirituality will continue to develop and reflect the Self that we are continually becoming when play is an integral part of our own being.

Notes

1. Peter L. Berger, *A Rumor of Angels* (New York: Doubleday and Company, 1969), p. 73.
2. C.G. Jung, *Letters*, Vol. 2: 1951–1961, ed. Gerhard Adler and Aniela Jaffe, trans. R.F.C. Hull (Princeton University Press, 1953–1975), p. 25.
3. C.G. Jung, *The Archetypes and the Collective Unconscious*, trans. R.F.C. Hull (New York: Bollingen Press, 1980), p. 164.
4. *Ibid.*
5. Berger, *A Rumor of Angels*, p. 73.
6. William J. Bouwsma, "Christian Adulthood," *Adulthood*, ed. Erik H. Erikson (New York: W.W. Norton Company, 1978), p. 81.
7. Gregory Baum, *Man Becoming* (New York: A Crossroad Book, Seabury Press, 1979), p. 154.
8. Hugo Rahner, *Man at Play* (New York: Herder and Herder, 1967), p. 65.
9. Harvey Cox, *Feast of Fools*, (Cambridge: Harvard University Press, 1969), p. 146.
10. Pierre Teilhard De Chardin, *The Divine Milieu* (New York: Harper and Row, 1960), p. 80.
11. Gregory Baum, *The Man Becoming* (New York: Herder and Herder, 1970; New York: A Crossroad Book, Seabury Press, 1979), p. 90.
12. C.G. Jung, *Letters*, p. 28.
13. William A. Sadler, Jr., "Creative Existence: Play as a Pathway to Personal Freedom and Community," *Humanitas*, Vol. 5, Personality and Play, Spring 1969, p. 75.

14. Russell A. Lockhart, "Psyche in Hiding," *Quadrant*, Spring 1980, p. 78.

15. C.G. Jung, *Memories, Dreams and Reflections*, Ed. Aniela Jaffe, trans. Richard and Clara Winston (New York: Vintage Books Edition, 1965), pp. 197–198.

16. *Ibid.*, pp. 198–199.

17. Dietrich Bonhoffer, *Letters and Papers from Prison* (London: S.C.M. Press, 1967), p. 187.

18. Hans Küng, *On Being A Christian*, trans. Edward Quinn (New York: Doubleday and Company Inc., 1976), p. 573.

19. Carl G. Jung, *Aion*, Collected Works, Vol. 9, Part II, trans. R.F.C. Hull (New York: Bollingen Foundation Inc., 1959; New Jersey: Princeton Press, 1980), p. 37.

20. *Ibid.*, p. 36.

21. Hans Küng, *On Being a Christian*, p. 545.

22. *Ibid.*, p. 572.

23. *Ibid.*, p. 602.

24 Carl G. Jung, *Integration of the Personality*, trans. Stanley Dell (New York: Farrar and Rinehart, Inc., 1939), p. 298.

BIBLIOGRAPHY

1. INDIVIDUATION AS A LIFE GOAL

Analytical Psychology Club of New York. *Carl Gustav Jung 1875–1961.* A Memorial Meeting, New York, Dec. 1, 1961. New York: Analytical Psychology Club of New York, Inc., 1962.

Carroll, James. "The Tumbler and the Princess", *Wonder and Worship.* New York: Paulist Press, 1976.

Conn, Walter E., editor, *Conversion.* New York: Alba House, 1978.

de Laszlo, Violet. "Preface," *Psyche and Symbol: A Selection from the Writings of C.G. Jung,* edited by Violet de Laszlo. New York: Doubleday and Company, Anchor Books, 1958.

Edinger, Edward F. *Ego and Archetype Individuation and the Religious Function of the Psyche.* New York: G.P. Putnam's Sons, 1972. Maryland: Penguin Books Inc., 1973.

Gould, Roger L. *Transformations.* New York: Simon and Schuster, 1978.

Hannah, Barbara. *Striving Toward Wholeness.* New York: G. P. Putnam's Sons, 1971.

Harding, M. Esther. *Journey into Self.* New York: David McKay Company, Inc., 1956.

Hiltner, Seward. "Toward A Theology of Conversion in the Light of Psychology," *Conversion,* edited by Walter E. Conn, Ph.D. New York: Alba House, 1978.

Jacobi, Jolande. *The Way of Individuation,* translated by R.F.C. Hull. Zurich: Rascher & Cie. A. G., 1965; New York: Harcourt Brace and World, 1967; England: Hodder and Stoughton Limited.

———. *The Psychology of C.G. Jung.* 7th ed. New Haven: Yale University Press, 1968.

Jaffe, Aniela. *The Myth of Meaning,* translated by R.F.C. Hull. New York: G.P. Putnam's Sons, 1971; Penguin Books, 1975.

Johnson, Paul E. *Psychology of Religion.* Nashville–New York: Whitmore and Stone, 1945; Abingdon Press, 1959.

Jung, C. G. *Aion.* Collected Works, Vol. 9, Part 2, translated by R.F.C. Hull. New York: Bollingen Foundation Inc., 1959. New Jersey: Princeton Press, 1979.

———. *The Archetypes and the Collective Unconscious.* Collected Works, Vol 9, Part 1, translated by R.F.C. Hull. New York: Bollingen Foundation Inc., 1959. New Jersey: Princeton Press, 1980.

———. *The Integration of the Personality,* translated by Stanley Dell. New York: Farrar and Rinehart, Inc., 1939.

———. *Memories, Dreams, Reflections,* translated by Richard and Clara Winston, recorded and edited by Aniela Jaffe. Revised Edition. New York: Random House, 1961; Vintage Books Paperback 1965.

———. *Modern Man in Search of a Soul,* translated by W.S. Dell and Cary F. Baynes. New York: Harvest Book/Harcourt, Brace and World Inc., 1933.

———. *Mysterium Coniunctionis,* Collected Works, Vol. 14, translated by R.F.C. Hull. New York: Bollingen Foundation Inc., 1963. New Jersey: First Princeton/Bollingen Paperback, 1977.

———. *Psychological Types,* Collected Works, Vol. 6, translated by H. G. Baynes and revised by R.F.C. Hull. New Jersey: Princeton University 1971, New Jersey: Bollingen Paperback, 1976.

———. *Psychology and Religion.* New Haven: Yale University Press, 1938.

———. *The Undiscovered Self,* translated by R.F.C. Hull. New York: New American Library, A Mentor Book, 1957.

———. *Two Essays on Analytical Psychology,* translated by R.F.C. Hull, second edition. Bollingen Series XX. The Collected Works of C. G. Jung, Vol. 7. Princeton University Press, 1966.

Levinson, Daniel J. (with Darrow, Charlotte N.; Klein, Edward B.; Levinson, Maria H.; McKee, Braxton), *The Seasons of a Man's Life.* New York: Knopf, 1978.

Lonergan, Bernard. "Theology in Its New Context," *Conversion,* edited by Walter E. Conn, Ph.D. New York: Alba House, 1978.

McCormick, Fowler, *Carl Gustav Jung 1875–1961. A Memorial Meeting*, New York, Dec. 1, 1961, Editors Analytical Psychology Club of New York, Inc., 1962, pp. 4–16.

O'Collins, Gerald. *The Second Journey*. New York: Paulist Press, 1978.

Pasquier, Jacques. "Experience and Conversion," *Conversion*, edited by Walter E. Conn Ph.D. New York: Alba House, 1978.

Phillips, Dorothy Berkley, ed. *The Choice is Always Ours: An Anthology on the Religious Way*. New York: Richard R. Smith, 1948.

Sanford, John. *The Invisible Partners*. New York: Paulist Press, 1980.

Singer, June. *Boundaries of The Soul*. New York: Doubleday, 1972. Anchor Books Paperback Edition, 1973.

Straude, John-Raphael. *The Adult Development of C.G. Jung*. Boston: Routledge and Kegan Paul, 1981.

Tillich, Paul. *The Courage To Be*. New Haven: Yale University Press, 1952.

Ulanov, Ann Belford. *The Feminine in Jungian Psychology and in Christian Spirituality*. Evanston: Northwestern University Press, 1971.

Von Franz, Marie Louise. *C.G. Jung: His Myth in Our Time*, translated by William H. Kennedy. Switzerland: Verlag Huber and Co. A. G., 1972; Boston: Little Brown and Co., 1975.

Whitmont, Edward C. *The Symbolic Quest*. Princeton: Princeton University Press, 1969.

Zeller, Max. "Some Aspects of the Individuation Process," *Paper Number 10*. Los Angeles: The Analytical Psychology Club of Los Angeles Inc., May 1960.

2. THE UNCONSCIOUS IN THE PERSONALITY THEORY OF CARL JUNG

de Laszlo, Violet. "Preface," *Psyche and Symbol. A Selection from the Writings of C.G. Jung*, edited by Violet de Laszlo. New York: Doubleday and Company Anchor Books, 1958.

Edinger, Edward F. *Ego and Archetype Individuation and the Religious Function of the Psyche*. New York: G.P. Putnam's Sons, 1972; Maryland: Penguin Books Inc., 1973.

Evans, Richard I. *Jung on Elementary Psychology. A Discussion Between C.G. Jung and Richard I. Evans.* New York: E.P. Dutton and Co., Inc. 1964; A Dutton Paperback, 1976.

Groesbeck, C. Jess. "The Analyst's Myth: Freud and Jung as Each Other's Analyst" *Quadrant*, Spring 1980, pp. 28–55.

Hall, Calvin S. and Nordby, Vernon J. *A Primer of Jungian Psychology.* New York: New American Library–Mentor, 1973.

Jacobi, Jolande. *Complex, Archetype, Symbol in the Psychology of C.G. Jung,* translated by Ralph Manheim. New Jersey: Princeton University Press, 1959, Bollingen Series LVII.

———. *The Psychology of C.G. Jung.* New Haven: Yale University Press, 1962.

Jaffe, Aniela. *The Myth of Meaning,* translated by R.F.C. Hull. New York: G.P. Putnam's Sons, 1971; Penguin Books, 1975.

Jones, Earnest. *The Life and Work of Sigmund Freud.* New York: Basic Books, 1955.

Jung, C. G. *Aion.* Collected Works, Vol. 9, Part 2, translated by R. F.C. Hull. New York: Bollingen Foundation Inc., 1959. New Jersey: Princeton Press, 1979.

———. *Analytical Psychology: Its Theory and Practice.* The Travistock Lecture. London: Routledge and Kegan Paul Ltd., 1968.

———. *Civilization in Transition,* translated by R.F.C. Hull, Bollingen Series XX. New Jersey: Princeton University Press, 1964.

———. *Man and His Symbols* (editor). New York: Doubleday Windfall Book, 1964.

———. *Memories, Dreams, Reflections,* translated by Richard and Clara Winston, recorded and edited by Aniela Jaffe. Revised Edition. New York: Random Books Paperback, 1965.

———. *Modern Man in Search of a Soul,* translated by W.S. Dell and Cary F. Baynes. New York: Harvest Book/Harcourt, Brace and World Inc., 1933.

———. *Mysterium Coniunctionis.* Collected Works, Vol. 14, translated by R.F.C. Hull. New York: Bollingen Foundation Inc., 1963. New Jersey: First Princeton Bollingen Paperback, 1977.

———. *On The Nature of the Psyche,* translated by R.F.C. Hull. Bollingen Series, New Jersey: Princeton University Press, 1960; third printing, 1973.

———. *Psychological Types*. Collected Works, Vol. 6, translated by H.G. Baynes and revised by R.F.C. Hull. New Jersey: Bollingen Paperback, 1976.

———. *Psychology and Religion*. New Haven: Yale University Press, 1938.

———.*the Archetypes and the Collective Unconscious*. Collected Works, Vol. 9, Part 1, translated by R.F.C. Hull. New York: Bollingen Foundation Inc., 1959. New Jersey: Princeton Press, 1980.

———. "The Spirit of Psychology," *This Is My Philosophy*, edited by Whit Burnett. New York: Harper and Brothers, 1959.

———. *The Undiscovered Self*. Translated by R.F.C. Hull. New York: New American Library, A Mentor Book, 1957.

———. *Two Essays on Analytical Psychology*, translated by R.F.C. Hull. Second Edition, Bollingen Series XX. The Collected Works of C.G. Jung, Vol. 7. Princeton, New Jersey: Princeton University Press, 1966.

Küng, Hans. *Freud and the Problem of God*. New Haven: Yale University Press, 1979.

Lockhart, Russell A. "Psyche in Hiding," *Quadrant*, Spring 1980, pp. 76–105.

Progoff, Ira. *Depth Psychology and Modern Man*. New York: McGraw-Hill Book Co., 1959.

———. *Jung, Synchronicity, and Human Destiny*. New York: Dell Publishing Co./A Delta Book, 1973.

Sanford, John. *The Invisible Partners*. New York: Paulist Press, 1980.

Schultz, Duane. *Theories of Personality*. Monterey, California: Brooks/ Cole Publishing Co., Wadsworth, 1976.

Ulanov, Ann and Barry. *Religion and the Unconscious*. Philadelphia: Westminster Press, 1975.

Von Franz, Marie Louise. *C.G. Jung: His Myth in Our Time*, translated by William H. Kennedy. Switzerland: Verlag Huber and Co. A. G., 1972; Boston: Little Brown and Co., 1975.

———. and Hillman, James. *Lectures on Jung's Typology*. Switzerland: Spring Publications, 1971.

Whitmont, Edward C. *The Symbolic Quest*. New Jersey: Princeton University Press, 1969.

3. PRAYER AND THE UNCONSCIOUS IN THE SECOND HALF OF LIFE

Bonny, Helen L. and Savary, Louis M. *Music and Your Mind.* New York: Harper and Row, 1973.

Brennan, Anne. "Myth in Personal Spirituality," *Religious Education,* Vol. 75, July–August 1980, pp. 441–451.

Brewi, Janice and Brennan, Anne. *Mid-Life: Psychological and Spiritual Perspectives.* New York: Crossroad, 1982.

Evans, Richard I. *Jung on Elementary Psychology. A Discussion Between C.G. Jung and I. Evans.* New York: E.P. Dutton and Co. Inc., 1976.

Farrell, Edward J., S.T.L. *Surprised by the Spirit.* New Jersey: Dimension Books, 1973.

Fourez, Gerald S.J. *A Sensible Guide to Prayer.* Chicago: Claretian Publications, 1973.

Fowler, James W. "Toward a Developmental Perspective on Faith," *Religious Education,* Vol. LXIX, March–April 1974, No. 2, pp. 207–218.

———. *Stages of Faith.* San Francisco: Harper and Row, 1981.

Fox, Matthew. *On Becoming a Musical Mystical Bear. Spirituality American Style.* New York: Paulist Press, 1972.

Fromm, Eric. *Greatness and Limitations of Freud's Thought.* New York: A Mentor Book, 1981.

Gelpi, Donald L., S.J. *Experiencing God.* New York: Paulist Press, 1978.

Gendlin, Eugene. *Focusing.* New York: Everest House, 1978.

Godin, André, S.J., editor. *From Cry to Word: Contributions Toward a Psychology of Prayer.* Belgium: Lumen Vitae Press, 1968.

Graham, Dom Aelred. *Zen Catholicism.* New York: Harcourt Brace and World, Inc., 1963.

Gray, Donald. "Passing Over and Coming Back," *Worship* 48, May 1974, pp. 300–304.

Greeley, Andrew. *Ecstasy: A Way of Knowing.* New Jersey: Prentice-Hall Inc., A Spectrum Book, 1974.

Happold, F.C. *The Journey Inward.* Atlanta: John Knox Press, 1968.

Harding, Esther M. *The I and the Not I.* New Jersey: Princeton University Press, 1965. Bollingen Paperback Edition, 1973.

James, William. *The Varieties of Religious Experience*. New York: Collier Books, Macmillan, 1961.

Johnston, William. *The Inner Eye of Love*. San Francisco: Harper and Row, 1978.

Jung, Carl G. *Modern Man in Search of a Soul*, translated by W.S. Dell and Cary F. Baynes. New York: Harvest Book, Harcourt, Brace and World, Inc., 1933.

———. *Psychology and Religion*. New Haven: Yale University Press, 1968.

———. *Psyche and Symbol*, edited by Violet de Laszlo. New York: Doubleday and Company, Anchor Book, 1958.

Kane, Thomas A. *The Healing Touch of Affirmation*. Massachusetts: Affirmation Books, 1976.

Kelsey, Morton. *The Other Side of Silence*. New York: Paulist Press, 1976.

Leech, Kenneth. *Soul Friend*. San Francisco: Harper and Row, 1980.

LeSaux, Henri, O.S.B. *Prayer (Abhishiktananda)*. Philadelphia: The Westminster Press, 1967.

LeShan, Lawrence. *How To Meditate*. Boston: Little Brown and Co., 1974; New York: Bantam Books, 1975.

Link, Mark, S.J. *You*. Illinois: Argus Communications, 1976.

Lynch, William F., S.J. *Images of Faith (An Explanation of Ironic Imagination)*. Notre Dame: University of Notre Dame, 1973.

May, Gerald G. *The Open Way* (A Meditation Handbook). New York: Paulist Press, 1977.

McDonagh, John M. *Christian Psychology*. New York: Crossroad, 1982.

Merton, Thomas. *Contemplation in a World of Action*. New York: Image Books, A Division of Doubleday, 1973.

Moltmann, Jurgen. *Experience of God*. Philadelphia: Fortress Press, 1980.

Murphy, Joseph. *The Power of Your Subconscious Mind*. New Jersey: Prentice-Hall Inc., 1963; New York: Bantam Books, 1982.

Progoff, Ira. *The Well and the Cathedral*. New York: Dialogue House Library, 1972, second edition enlarged, 1977.

Rahner, Karl, S.J. *On Prayer*. New York: Paulist Press, 1968.

Rahner, Karl and Metz, Johann B. *The Courage To Pray*. New York: Crossroad, 1981.

Savary, Louis M. and Berne, Patricia H. *Prayerways*. San Francisco: Harper and Row, 1980.

Sheets, John, S.J. *The Spirit Speaks in Us*. New Jersey: Dimension Books, 1969.

Stahl, Carolyn. *Opening to God (Guided Imagery Meditation on Scripture)*. Nashville: The Upper Room, 1977.

Ulanov, Ann Belford. *The Feminine in Jungian Psychology and in Christian Spirituality*. Evanston: Northwestern University Press, 1971.

Ulanov, Ann and Barry. *Religion and the Unconscious*. Philadelphia: Westminister Press, 1975.

Wink, Walter. *The Bible in Human Transformation*. Philadelphia: Fortress Press, 1973.

Woods, Richard, O.P., ed. *Understanding Mysticism*. New York: Image Books, A Division of Doubleday, 1980.

4. THE SHADOW IN THE PERSONALITY THEORY OF CARL JUNG

Detloff, Wayne. "Psychological Types: Fifty Years After," *Psychological Perspectives*, Vol. 3, 1972.

Fierz-David, Linda. *Notes on the Psychological Types*, an unpublished manuscript, 1949.

Fordham, Frieda. *An Introduction to Jung's Psychology*. New York: Penguin Books. 1953.

Fordham, Michael. "Notes on Psychological Types," *Journal of Analytical Psychology*, Vol. 17, 1972.

Gray, Horace, Wheelwright, Joseph, and Wheelwright, Jane. *Jungian Type Survey*. San Francisco: Society of Jungian Analysts, 1943.

Groesbeck, C.J. "Psychological Types in the Analysis of Transference," *Journal of Analytical Psychology*, Vol. 23, 1978.

Harding, M. Esther. *The I and the Not I: A Study in the Development of Consciousness*. New Jersey: Princeton University Press. Bollingen Series LXXIX, 1965.

Jacobi, Jolande. *The Way of Individuation*, translated by R.F.C. Hull. Zurich: Roscher and Cie. A.G., 1965; New York: Harcourt Brace and World, 1967.

Jung, C.G. *Aion*, translated by R.F.C. Hull. New Jersey: Princeton University Press. Bollingen Series XX, 1959.

———. *Analytical Psychology: Its Theory and Practice.* The Travistock Lectures. London: Routledge and Kegan Paul Ltd., 1968.

———.*Letters.* Vol. 1: 1906–1950, edited by Gerhard Adler and Aniella Jaffe, translated by R.F.C. Hull. New Jersey: Princeton University Press, 1973.

———.*Letters.* Vol. 2: 1951–1961, edited by Gerhard Adler and Aniela Jaffe, translated by R.F.C. Hull. New Jersey: Princeton University Press, 1953–1975.

———.*Man and His Symbols* (editor). New York: Doubleday Windfall Book, 1964.

———.*Mysterium Coniunctionis.* Collected Works, Vol. 14, translated by R.F.C. Hull. New York: Bollingen Foundation Inc., 1963.

———. *Psychological Types.* Collected Works, Vol. 6, translated by H.G. Baynes and revised by R.F.C. Hull. New Jersey: Princeton University Press, 1971.

Kiersey, David and Bates, Marilyn. *Please Understand Me.* Del Mar, California: Prometheus Nemesis Books, 1978.

Marshall, I.N. "The Four Functions, A Conceptional Analysis," *Journal of Analytical Psychology,* Vol. 13, 1968.

Miller, William A. *Why Do Christians Break Down?* Minneapolis: Augsburg Press, 1973.

Myers, Isabel Briggs and Myers, Peter B. *Gifts Differing.* California: Consulting Psychological Press Inc., 1980.

Sanford, John A. *Evil: The Shadow Side of Reality.* New York: Crossroad, 1981.

Singer, June. *Boundaries of the Soul.* New York: Doubleday, 1972.

Von Franz, Marie-Louise and Hillman, James. *Lectures on Jung's Typology.* Zurich: Spring Publications, 1971.

———.*Shadow and Evil in Fairytales.* New York: Spring Publications, 1974.

Wheelwright, Joseph and Bradway, Kathleen. "Psychological Types," *Journal of Analytical Psychology,* Vol. 23, 1978.

———."Critical Notes on Jung's Psychological Types," *Journal of Analytical Psychology,* Vol. 17, 1972.

Whitmont, Edward D. *The Symbolic Quest.* New Jersey: Princeton University Press, 1969.

5. THE SHADOW AND PRAYER IN THE SECOND HALF OF LIFE

Campbell, Joseph. *Myths to Live By.* New York: Bantam Books, 1973.

Doran, Robert M., S.J. "Jungian Psychology and Christian Spirituality: I," *Review for Religious,* Volume 38, No. 4, pp. 407–510.

———."Jungian Psychology and Christian Spirituality: II," *Review for Religious,* Volume 38, No. 5, pp. 742–752.

———."Jungian Psychology and Christian Spirituality: III, *Review for Religious,* Volume 38, No. 6, pp. 857–866.

Fairchild, Roy W. *Finding Hope Again: A Pastor's Guide to Counseling Depressed Persons.* San Francisco: Harper and Row, 1980.

Fittipaldi, Silvio. *How To Pray Always Without Always Praying.* Notre Dame: Fides/Claretian, 1978.

Gelpi, Donald L., S.J. *Experiencing God.* New York: Paulist Press, 1978.

Gould, Roger L. *Transformations.* New York: Simon and Schuster, 1978.

Jung, C.G. *Aion.* Collected Works, Volume 9, Part II, translated by R.F.C. Hull. New York: Bollingen Foundation Inc., New Jersey: Princeton University Press, 1979.

———.*Answer to Job,* in *The Portable Jung,* edited by Joseph Campbell, translated by R.F.C. Hull. New York: Penguin Books, 1977.

———.*Man and His Symbols* (editor). New York: Doubleday Windfall Book, 1964.

———.*Memories, Dreams and Reflections,* edited by Aniela Jaffe, translated by Richard and Clara Winston. New York: Vantage Books, 1965.

———.*Psychology and Religion: West and East,* Volume II, Collected Works, translated by R.F.C. Hull. New Jersey: Princeton University Press, 1969.

Kelsey, Morton. *Discernment A Study in Ecstasy and Evil.* New York: Paulist Press, 1978.

———.*The Other Side of Silence.* New York: Paulist Press, 1976.

Lane, Dermot A. *The Reality of Jesus.* New York: Paulist Press, 1975.

Leech, Kenneth. *Soul Friend.* San Francisco: Harper and Row, 1977.

Levinson, Daniel. *The Seasons of a Man's Life.* New York: Knopf, 1978.

Linn, Dennis, S.J. and Linn, Matthew, S.J. *Healing Life's Hurts.* New York: Paulist Press, 1978.

Lynch, William. *Images of Hope.* Notre Dame: University of Notre Dame Press, 1974.

McNutt, Francis. *The Power To Heal.* Notre Dame: Ave Maria Press, 1977.

Miller, William A. *Make Friends with Your Shadow.* Minneapolis: Augsburg Press, 1981.

O'Connor, Elizabeth. *Our Many Selves.* New York: Harper and Row, 1971.

Sanford, John A. *Evil: The Shadow Side of Reality.* New York: Crossroad, 1981.

———. *The Kingdom Within.* New York: J.P. Lippincottt Company, 1970.

Shea, John. *Stories of God.* Chicago: The Thomas More Press, 1978.

Teresa of Avila. *Interior Castle,* translated and edited by E. Allison Peers. New York: Image Books, A Division of Doubleday, 1961.

Ulanov, Ann and Barry. *Primary Speech: A Psychology of Prayer,* Atlanta: John Knox Press, 1982.

———. *Religion and the Unconscious.* Philadelphia: The Westminster Press, 1975.

Watts, Alan W. *Myth and Ritual In Christianity.* Boston: Beacon Press, 1968.

Welch, John, O. Carm. *Spiritual Pilgrims: Carl Jung and Teresa of Avila.* New York: Paulist Press, 1982.

Williams, Strephon Kaplan. *Jungian-Senoi Dreamwork Manual.* Berkeley: Journey Press, 1980.

6. TOWARD A DEFINITION OF PLAY

B.B.C. television documentary. *The Story of Carl Gustav Jung with Commentary by Laurens Van der Post.* Produced by Jonathan Stendall. Filmed in 1971.

Berger, Peter L. *A Rumor of Angels.* New York: Doubleday and Co., 1969.

Bolles, Richard N. *The Three Boxes of Life.* Berkeley: Ten Speed Press, 1978.

Bouwsma, William J. "Christian Adulthood," *Adulthood,* ed. Erik H. Erikson. New York: W.W. Norton, 1978, pp. 81–96.

Clinebell, Howard. *Growth Counseling.* Nashville: Abingdon, 1979.

———. *Growth Counseling for Mid-Years Couples.* Philadelphia: Fortress Press, 1977.

Cousins, Norman. "Anatomy of an Illness (As Perceived by the Patient," *The Healing Continuum,* ed. Patricia Ann Flynn. Maryland: Robert J. Brady Co., a Prentice-Hall Publishing, 1980, pp. 375–387.

Dunne, John S. *Time and Myth.* New York: Doubleday and Co., 1973. Reprint ed. Notre Dame: Notre Dame University Press, 1975.

Fingarette, Herbert. "All Play and No Work," *Humanitas,* Vol. 5: Personality and Play (Spring 1969), pp. 5–19.

Flynn, Patricia Anne Randolph. *Holistic Health.* Maryland: Robert J. Brady Co., a Prentice-Hall Publishing, 1980.

Fowler, Jim, and Keen, Sam. *Life Maps,* ed. Jerome Berryman. Texas: Word Books, 1978.

Friedman, Meyer, M.D., and Rosenman, Ray H., M.D. *Type A Behavior and Your Heart.* Connecticut: Fawcett Publications Inc. (paperback ed.), 1974.

Greeley, Andrew. *Ecstasy: A Way of Knowing.* New Jersey: Prentice-Hall Inc., a Spectrum Book, 1974.

———.*Love and Play.* New York: Seabury Press, 1977.

Harding, M. Esther. *The I and the Not I.* Princeton, New Jersey: Princeton University Press, 1965; Bollingen paperback ed., 1973.

Hein, Hilde. "Play as an Aesthetic Concept," *Humanitas,* Vol. 5: Personality and Play (Spring 1969), pp. 57–80.

Huizinga, Johan. *Homo Ludens: A Study of the Play Element in Culture,* tr. R.F.C. Hull, Boston: Beacon Press, 1955.

Keen, Sam. *Beginnings Without End.* New York: Harper and Row, 1977.

Kiersey, David, and Bates, Marilyn. *Please Understand Me.* Del Mar, California: Prometheus Nemesis Books, 1978.

Maslow, Abraham H. "Lessons From the Peak Experiences," *Journal of Humanistic Psychology,* Vol. 11, No. 1 (1962), 9–18.

———. *Religions, Values and Peak-Experiences.* New York: Viking Press, 1970 (1964 by Kappa Delta Pi), fifth printing, 1972.

May, Rollo. *The Courage To Create.* New York: Bantam Books/W.W. Norton and Co., 1st ed., 1975, fifth printing, 1978.

McGlashan, Alan. *Gravity and Levity.* Boston: Houghton-Mifflin Co., 1976.

Millar, Susanna. *The Psychology of Play.* New York: Jason Aronson, 1974.

Moran, Gabriel. *Education Toward Adulthood.* New York: Paulist Press, 1979.

Myers, Isabel Briggs, and Myers, Peter B. *Gifts Differing.* California: Consulting Psychologist Press, Inc., 1980.

Sadler, William A., Jr. "Creative Existence: Play as a Pathway to Personal Freedom and Community," *Humanitas,* Vol. 5: Personality and Play (Spring 1969), pp. 57–58.

———. "Play: A Basic Human Structure Involving Love and Freedom," *Review of Existential Psychology and Psychiatry,* Fall 1966, 237–245.

Savary, Louis M. *Man: His World and His Work.* New York: Paulist Press, 1967.

Toffler, Alvin. *The Third Wave.* New York: Bantam Books/William Morrow and Co., 1st ed., 1979, Bantam ed. 1981.

Varga, Ivan. "Capitalism and the Return to Religion," *The Ecumenist* (May–June 1980), 54–59.

Watts, Alan. *Nature, Man and Woman.* New York: Vintage Books, 1970.

7. INDIVIDUATION AND PLAY

Analytical Psychology Club of New York. Carl Gustav Jung 1875–1961. *A Memorial Meeting,* New York, Dec. 1, 1961. New York: Analytical Psychology Club of New York, Inc., 1962.

Berger, Peter. *A Rumor of Angels.* New York: Doubleday and Company, 1969.

Clinebell, Howard. *Growth Counseling,* Nashville: Abingdon, 1979.

Dangott, Lillian R. and Kalish, Richard A. *A Time To Enjoy.* New Jersey; Prentice-Hall Inc., 1979.

Dunne, John S. *Time and Myth*. New York: Doubleday and Company, 1973; reprint ed. Notre Dame: Notre Dame University Press, 1975.

Greeley, Andrew M. *Ecstasy: A Way of Knowing*. New Jersey: Prentice-Hall Inc., 1974.

Jung, C.G. *Aion*, Collected Works Vol. 9, Part 2, translated by R.F.C. Hull. New York: Bollingen Foundation Inc., 1959. New Jersey: Princeton University Press, 1979.

———. *Letters*. Vol. 2: 1959–1961, edited by Gerhard Adler and Aniela Jaffe, translated by R.F.C. Hull. Princeton: Princeton University Press, 1953–.

———.*Letters*. Vol. 1: 1906–1950, edited by Gerhard Adler and Aniela Jaffe, translated by R.F.C. Hull. Princeton: Princeton University Press, 1973.

———.*Man and His Symbols* (editor). New York: Doubleday Windfall Book, 1964.

———.*Memories, Dreams, Reflections*, translated by Richard and Clara Winston, recorded and edited by Aniela Jaffe. Revised Edition. New York: Random House, 1961; Vintage Books Paperback, 1965.

———.*On the Nature of the Psyche*, translated by R.F.C. Hull. Bollingen Series. New Jersey: Princeton University Press, 1960. Third Printing, 1973.

———.*The Integration of the Personality*, translated by Stanley Dell. New York: Farrar and Rinehart, Inc., 1939.

Lindberg, Anne Morrow. *Gift from the Sea*. New York: Vintage Books Edition, 1978.

Lionni, Leo. *Frederick*. New York: Random House Pantheon Books, 1967.

McGlashan, Alan. *Gravity and Levity*. Boston: Houghton Mifflin Company, 1976.

Von Franz, Marie Louise and Hillman, James. *Lectures on Jung's Typology*. Switzerland: Spring Publications, 1971.

8. PLAY AND PERSONAL SPIRITUALITY

Baum, Gregory. *Man Becoming*. New York: Herder and Herder Inc., 1970. New York: A Crossroad Book, paperback, Seabury Press, 1979.

Berger, Peter. *A Rumor of Angels*. New York: Doubleday and Company, 1969.

Bonhoffer, Dietrich. *Letters and Papers from Prison*. London: S.C.M. Press, 1967.

Bouwsma, William J. "Christian Adulthood," *Adulthood*, edited by Erik H. Erikson. New York: W.W. Norton Co., 1978, pp. 81–96.

Clinebell, Howard J. *Growth Counseling for Mid-Years Couples*. Philadelphia: Fortress Press, 1977.

Cox, Harvey. *The Feast of Fools*. Cambridge: Harvard University Press, 1969.

Gill, Jean. *Images of My Self*. New York: Paulist Press, 1982.

Greeley, Andrew M. *Ecstasy—A Way of Knowing*. New Jersey: Prentice-Hall Inc., 1974.

———. *Love and Play*. New York: Seabury Press, 1977.

Jung, C.G. *Aion*, Collected Works, Vol. 9, Part II, translated by R.F.C. Hull New York: Bollingen Foundation Inc., 1959. New Jersey: Princeton Press, 1980.

———. *The Archetypes and the Collective Unconscious*, Vol. 9, Part I, translated by R.F.C. Hull. New York: Bollingen Foundation Inc., 1959. New Jersey: Princeton Press, 1980.

———. *Letters*. Vol. I: 1906–1950, edited by Gerhard Adler and Aniela Jaffe, translated by R.F.C. Hull. Princeton: Princeton University Press, 1973.

——— *Letters*. Vol II: 1951–1961, edited by Gerhard Adler and Aniela Jaffe, translated by R.F.C. Hull. Princeton: Princeton University Press, 1953–1975.

———. *Memories, Dreams and Reflections*, edited by Aniela Jaffe, translated by Richard and Clara Winston. New York: Vintage Books edition, 1965.

———. *The Integration of the Personality*. translated by Stanley Dell. New York: Farrar and Rinehart, Inc., 1939.

Keen, Sam. *Beginnings Without End*. New York: Harper and Row, 1977.

Küng, Hans. *On Being a Christian*, translated by Edward Quinn. New York: Doubleday and Company Inc., 1976.

Lockhart, Russell A. "Psyche in Hiding," *Quadrant*, Spring 1980, pp. 76–105.

Rahner, Hugo. *Man at Play*. New York: Herder and Herder, 1967.

Sadler, Jr., William A. "Creative Existence: Play as a Pathway to

Personal Freedom and Community,"*Humanitas,* Vol. 5, Personality and Play, Spring 1969, pp. 57–80.

Teilhard De Chardin, Pierre. *The Divine Milieu.* New York: Harper and Row, 1960.

Toffler, Alvin, "A New Kind of Man in the Making," *The New York Times Magazine,* March 9, 1980, pp. 24–30.

Van Kaam, Adrian: *Spirituality and the Gentle Life.* New Jersey: Dimension Books, Inc., 1974.